THE MOST REV. EDWARD RALPH JOHNSON,
BISHOP OF CALCUTTA, 1876–98.

[*Frontispiece.*

A HISTORY OF THE OXFORD MISSION TO CALCUTTA

ORIGINALLY WRITTEN BY

GEORGE LONGRIDGE, B.A.

OF THE COMMUNITY OF THE RESURRECTION; SOMETIME VICAR OF GROVE, WANTAGE

AND NOW COMPLETED WITH AN ADDITIONAL
CHAPTER DOWN TO 1909

WITH A PREFACE BY THE
RIGHT REV. EDWARD STUART TALBOT, D.D.
LORD BISHOP OF SOUTHWARK

REVISED AND ABRIDGED FOR THE SECOND EDITION BY
W. H. HUTTON, B.D.,
FELLOW AND PRECENTOR OF S. JOHN'S COLLEGE, OXFORD

A. R. MOWBRAY & CO. LTD.
LONDON : 28 Margaret Street, Oxford Circus, W
OXFORD : 9 High Street
1910

TO

THE BRETHREN OF THE EPIPHANY

WHO HAVE THE COURAGE

NOT ONLY TO WORK

BUT TO WAIT

INTRODUCTORY NOTE

A NEW edition of the *History of the Oxford Mission to Calcutta* is called for at a time when public attention in England is being directed, in a special way, by political movements and by tragic events, to affairs in Bengal. To those who have studied India there is nothing surprising in what has happened or is happening. The words quoted in this book from a Bengali gentleman, written originally in 1896, have proved prophetic indeed. He summed up the complaint of Indian parents who saw the effects of English secular education on their children:

"You call this civilization, and are proud of having communicated its impact to India; but are you aware what mischief you are unwittingly doing us? Your scientific education has made our children irreligious, atheistic, agnostic; they are beginning to look upon religion as (what one of your clever writers called it the other day) 'a dream of hysterical women and half-starved men'; they no longer believe in the divine source of virtue, but think that it is a proper balancing of profit and loss; they have become irreverent, disobedient, disloyal; they have lost all fixity of character; they are too ready to act on the first prompting of passion and interest and call it independence; they boast that they have adopted the Epicurean precept, 'Eat, drink, and be merry, for to-morrow we die and become carbonic

v

acid, water, and ammonia'; and they laugh at us
old men for what they mockingly call our antediluvian notions. Surely the Iron Age has come,
for it has been said that when it comes knowledge
will be more and more, but wisdom will be less and
less. And that you Englishmen should be the
leaders of such an age is quite in accordance with
the fitness of things. You say you have given us
light, but your light is worse than darkness. We
do not thank you for it." And he said that, "whether
we agreed with the complaint or not, it was in-
disputable that a time of crisis was at hand. The
old religion is dying; the old morality is dying; the
bonds of custom and tradition which are the bones
and sinews of the social organism are dissolving;
there is death and decomposition all around. For
all this the secular spirit of the educational system
is responsible. The crisis is serious; the destiny of
a nation is at stake. A mere let-aloneist attitude will
not do; something must be done to replace that
which is passing away. If an attempt is made to
face the crisis with boldness, with promptitude, and
in right earnest, well and good; if not, matters will
soon become still more hopeless, the reins will have
been thrown upon the necks of the horses, and the
last hope of reform without revolution will be gone."

Those who are responsible for the Oxford Mission
to Calcutta, those who direct it and work in it in
India, those who work for it and pray for it in
England, feel that in its methods will be found the
true help in India's need. Calcutta seems now, as
the Bishop of Southwark tells us, writing just a

month ago, to be keenly alive; so it has always seemed to acute observers. New life is coming; so it has always seemed to the devout Hindu. We believe that CHRIST alone, in all the fullness of His message to man, can truly give them that life. And it has been the undeviating aim of the Oxford Mission, all these years, to present the Gospel in all its fullness, in sympathy with all the needs of human life, and all the highest aspirations of man. National progress in literature and religion will find their highest expression in the Church of CHRIST. So the Oxford Mission offers its patient work, and is ready—if it has the help that Christian England is bound, for very shame, to give it—to meet the needs of the new age, in the spirit of the LORD, the Lifegiver.

Those whose privilege it has been—as it was mine in 1901—to spend the Epiphany festival with the Community in Calcutta, will never forget how that happy day seems most fitly associated with the work of the Mission. The reality and fervour of the service, the number of devout worshippers, mostly natives, at the Eucharist, are signs of that full Epiphany which is to come.

The Oxford Mission is laying a sure foundation, and its members are working with all their hearts and all their strength. It is a work hard, disappointing—but certainly it is not disheartening. Of the many hearers there are as yet few indeed who become Christians; but I cannot forbear to quote some words of the Superior of the Community—words which, little though I know of India,

I know enough to feel certain are true :—" There remain the few to whom the Word of GOD comes home, as it has always come home to guileless souls. One by one they turn their faces towards the light, and by a longer or a shorter journey they eventually reach it. These few genuine and true converts are the real hope of India. Their influence and their numbers are steadily increasing—their influence more rapidly than their numbers. It is for us to watch over their growth with the tenderest care, to do all we can for them by helping them when they are in need, and by standing aside when they no longer want us. If we missionaries have the wisdom to guide them rightly now with our LORD'S own combination of helpfulness and reserve, we shall see, or our successors will see, a bold, independent, aggressive, native Christian Church, strong enough to do its own work of the conversion of India, strong in prayer, strong in charity, and, above all things, in character—winning, by its own inherent beauty, the love and admiration of all except those who really *love* darkness rather than light, because their deeds are evil." In this lies the promise of the Epiphany which is still to come in India.

Of the preparation it is that this book tells. By the wish of the Committee of the Oxford Mission, and the cordial sanction of the author, I have reduced the size of the original volume, so that it may be sold more cheaply, and have made a few necessary changes.

W. H. H.

Fourth Sunday in Lent, 1910.

PREFACE

I EARNESTLY desire for this little book a large audience and a thoughtful reception ; for it sets out in brief but sufficient outline one of the problems of England's Christian Empire, and tells of a tiny but invaluable effort towards its solution. The moment is timely for such matters. The voice of GOD through events and history is teaching English-men, as no words could ever teach, the lessons of Imperial responsibility. It drives home the questions why and for how long that Empire is given, what are its tasks, and what its true foundations and resources. The scope of such questions goes far beyond the particular case which suggests them. The lessons of Africa, and whatever quickening of national conscientiousness is gained there through sorrow and suffering, may show their effect in India. For India's is certainly the " leading case " in the list of English responsibilities. Nowhere else does the future rest, under GOD, so absolutely upon us, or seem charged with possibilities for good and evil so enormous. Nowhere is the appeal to the stronger nation and more robust civilization for parental care more urgent and pathetic.

Calcutta is but one corner of India, but, educationally as much as politically, it is a centre. Its educated class is but a fraction of India's enormous populations, but it is the fraction which is most directly susceptible of English influence, and which exercises the largest share of the power that belongs to speech and writing.

The case between us and this section of Indian life may be put into a nutshell : we must destroy ; shall we help to build up ? In view of our great administrative constructions, especially the educational organization, this way of putting the case may seem a paradox ; but it is not so to those who reflect that the first result of an inrush of foreign ideas, even if they were not the ideas of an advanced and critical civilization, would be to undermine and discredit and destroy many of the institutions and forces which have been the support and strength of a people's life. We have to recognize that " knowledge is power " only when it is wielded by a force greater than itself —that force is life, the higher or spiritual life of a people. In this sense, as in others, it is true that " the letter killeth, the Spirit giveth life." The strength of a nation's life comes from the faith that is in it. Now we must, by our education, do much to destroy India's faiths. As Christian Englishmen we believe that we have a better Faith to give, a Faith which, to speak only of its social influence, is of incomparably higher bonding power and wholesome effect. Shall we do this second and higher part of our work ? Shall we, I repeat, help to build up ? The Government cannot do this ; it can only give

the indirect testimony—which is indeed invaluable—
of a lofty and incorruptible justice and a humane
and moral administration in system and in *personnel*.
But the Church which speaks in the English tongue
can bear witness whence it was that England
received these great national blessings to impart to
her dependencies. The Church can speak freely and
without reserve of that faith in the true GOD and in
JESUS CHRIST Whom He hath sent, that faith in the
stooping of GOD and the lifting of man through
Him, to which England owes all that makes her
English best—not indeed its raw material, but its
moulding and building and preserving.

All this is set out, but far better and with the convincing effect of concrete experience and expert
testimony, in what follows (see, e.g., p. 79). The
upshot from the mouth of an Indian is expressed
(p. 81) in the words, " The destiny of a nation is at
stake. A mere let-aloneist attitude will not do."

But the book also contains a sketch of an attempt,
vigorous, faithful, and practical, to meet the problem
with an answer, and to turn these reflections into
action. The characteristic of the moment for England and her Church seems to be that the confront-
ing problems, at home and abroad, everywhere
outmatch and overmaster by their scale and area
and variety the resources for meeting them. The
proportionate size of this little island on the map of
the world is extraordinarily symbolical. But the
courage of Englishmen and, one would hope, in a
far deeper sense the faith of English Christians, do
not stop at difficulties. To have done what we

could must be everywhere the aim which animates
our efforts. A little community, originating in the
prayerful self-sacrifice of two or three men, though
claiming with happy audacity representative relation
with the greatest of English universities, is after all but
a drop in India's ocean of life. But there are drops,
spiritual as well as physical, of rare potency, and
I cannot but believe that this has been, and will be,
such an one. Faith and self-sacrifice, worship and
sympathy, keen and active respect for all the parts
and kinds of human faculty and knowledge, the
union and freedom of a fellowship or brotherhood
whose tie has been one of constraining reality while
always voluntary—these, which have been the every-
day equipment of the Oxford Mission to Calcutta,
would certainly seem to give promise of the truest
kind of work. Those to whom some forms of
missionary work have not appealed may find here
credentials which they can accept of first-class work.
They will notice the thorough belief in light (" It
is not the high, but the low standard of education
which is the danger," p. 145), the clear recognition
that moral and religious work are in the end one
(p. 99), the readiness, accordingly, to work patiently
through the one for a future harvest of the other (as
in the case of the Hostel for non-Christian students
—an oasis of pure life amidst corrupt surroundings,
pp. 82–89), the largeness of heart with which men
of strong dogmatic and ecclesiastical conviction
cordially invoke the Christian work of others on
their right and on their left to independent co-
operation in the same field. They will certainly

recognize the fine and magic touch of personal sympathy, the strength and still more the patience of its compassion and desire to help; and they will hardly miss the springs of this in an inner life of communion with GOD.

We speak best of what we know and to those by whom we are known. My own reverence for the work of the Oxford Mission to Calcutta is largely of the grateful sort. We Oxford men of those days felt that its start worked with the words of our most 'prophetic' teacher (for such we felt 'Dr. King' to be), to enlarge our horizon of intellectual and religious responsibility. Among surroundings of academical debate it taught us the reality, modern as ever, of spiritual power. Willis and Argles showed us fresh examples of simplicity in responding to inward vocation from GOD; and the life of Philip Smith was to some of us in Oxford, as to many not themselves Christians in Calcutta, a glimpse of the hem of the garment of JESUS CHRIST as He moved in the pure charm of divine simplicity and compassion among the sons of men, and the little children came to Him.

GOD grant that, whoever else neglects its quiet witness and its moving appeal, the voice of Oxford's own Mission in India may reach with gathering and constraining power some of Oxford's best sons in each succeeding generation of her life! One would like to hope that many a man whom Oxford has taught ambitions or ideals of noble living, and furnished with keen instruments for high work, without being able to show him how and when to realize the one and use the other, may find what he lacks at that little centre of Christian life and love in the capital of the great land of many nations which GOD has given to England, and may do work greater than can be reckoned for England's Empire and England's Church.

How long shall the call to shed their blood under England's flag, whatever the issue, or even to give their lives to English enterprise and administration, be heard so much more readily by her sons than the call to swell the first battalion (surely it is England's!) in the bloodless crusade of CHRIST, or to quicken, under GOD, the life of coming generations with the old germinant, fruitful seed of the Word of His Truth?

.   .   .   .   .

So far I wrote ten years ago, and in reading over my words, I hardly find any which I wish to alter. The thoughts which they contain have become more unmistakable platitudes; but they are not yet, I fear, commonplaces of action. I spoke then of a critical moment of opportunity; the interval has emphasized its critical character; and in some ways the opportunity is already abridged. The aspirations of the class at which the Mission directly aimed, the University students, are harder to guide towards faith, because they are now largely given away to political ideals. If there is any sentence which I should now write differently, it is the one in which I spoke of India's appeal to us for "parental care." I may, and do, believe, that England has still much that is "parental" to do for India, and that in Indian character there is much still, for good and evil, of the child that needs and welcomes help and guidance. But the other side of the matter has become more prominent. India in many of her sons, feels adult and confident and conscious of herself; they see more clearly what we lack, and what they have. The ideal before us must accordingly be more that of a sisterly than a parental relation; there must be exchange, and one must complement the other. We shall acknowledge that this is so even in the matter of religious life and character, so long as by the acknowledgement we do not do India the injury of abating or seeming to abate either the imperial claim of CHRIST to the sovereignty of all men, or the fullness of the message and witness about Him which we are bound to invite Indians to receive through us, till they can receive it, more widely than is yet possible, through men of their own colour and race.

But there are a few words which I should like to add to bring my preface up to date.

The first is a word of thankfulness and of admiration: of thankfulness to GOD for what He has done, and of admiration for what He has enabled His servants in this Mission to be and to do for Him. I have now seen for myself the Mission in its three centres; and can speak with the added confidence that comes from sight. The roots are deeper, the grasp surer, the resources greater. The work is beautiful work, and it is done with noble devotion, patience and persevering charity, and with

the brightness of quiet calm which comes upon work
so done. Let us who love the Mission give thanks
when we pray, and pray the better for doing so.

I pass naturally to a word of confidence and hope.
No supporter of the Mission need have any mis-
givings about the necessity and importance of its work.
There has been no doubt both failure and change.
The Mission has not accomplished all that it hoped
to do; and its energies are partly turned in new
directions. The work with students has not yet
yielded the results of direct conversion for which
we hoped. But the truth is happily more and more
recognized, that so long as we do our duty in efforts
of this kind, we must leave the issue to GOD without
complaining if results are delayed, or dictating what
they should be. This is true in a very marked
degree of such work as is attempted by the Oxford
Brethren. The time may come at any moment
when, in answer to their work, men may come out
by twos and threes to own CHRIST, and face all
that is implied in becoming Christians. But let no
one suppose that till that day comes the work is
only marking time. The outstanding feature of
Indian missionary work is the enormous strength
of its indirect results in the Christianizing of thought,
character, and conduct among those who still are
not Christians. The positive and present value of
this is in a moral way inestimable. The value of
it for the future in preparation of soil and atmosphere
may well be proved in the next generation by results
beyond all that we now imagine.

But the Mission, it may be said, has discreetly

acknowledged failure, and transferred its energies to more promising fields. The answer is that this is not true. What has happened is that there has been growth and development. Experience has shown, as so often before, that the spiritual forces are stronger than the intellectual : and that the Mission can do less by argument than by the manifestation of the spirit and power in the simpler ways of pastoral cares. Anyhow, such work has come to their hand, and they have responded to calls of divine providence and of authority. The old work has not indeed been abandoned—far from it. The house stands where it did, accessible to all the student life, and the Brethren who inhabit it keep touch with the students in many ways. *The Epiphany* maintains still its open lists for all comers, gives its terse, frank replies to questioners and correspondents, guides the thoughts of its many thousand Indian readers to necessary distinctions and clear thought about the things that are Christian. In the Hostel at Calcutta, and in the newer one at Dacca, there is daily intercourse with men of whom perhaps none are Christian : influence is gained, confidence is won, and, as I can testify, the witness of good effect is written on the faces of the men.

But to this has been added work in teaching the children, and in evangelizing and shepherding peasant congregations in the district round Barisal : a new enterprise of this kind is being begun by Mr. Douglass in Behala, a suburb of Calcutta. Above all, the association with the Brethren of a Sisterhood of ladies has produced at Barisal work of beautiful tenderness and fairest promise. Perhaps the latest of these developments is as interesting as any, and answers most nearly to some of our best hopes. It is the formation under one of the students of the Mission, ordained deacon last Christmas, and approved by the Bishop of Calcutta as one of his most competent candidates, of a band of Indian youths trained in the Barisal schools, who will carry on at their own enterprise, and without any remuneration, tasks of evangelization among the country people of the neighbourhood. The freshness and singleness of such work cannot fail, we think, to tell.

It is thus that there remains with me the conviction that the Mission is doing riper and fuller work as the years go on, still happily under the guidance of one of its very first members.

But there remains to be said a word of regret, I had almost said of reproach. If the intellectual work of the Brethren occupies to-day a proportionately smaller part, and falls short of what they and we desire, where are we to place the blame? Surely it is upon us at home that it must fall. Three or four years ago Mr. Teignmouth Shore, in a speech which made a great impression, told an Oxford audience that for seven years Oxford had not contributed to this Oxford Mission a single recruit, and though this would not now be true to the letter the position is substantially unchanged. The work of the Mission goes forward, but the specific appeal made by it, or rather by the opportunity which it strives to redeem, to the faith and zeal and churchmanship of Oxford is not as yet taken up. I wish I had the pen to bring home the stress of that appeal, and the critical importance of the issue. Indian life and Indian thought are all astir. There is no stagnation, no "unchanging East," now in Calcutta. The sense is keen that new things are coming, that a new life is in the making. What is to be the strength and what the wisdom for new constructions of thought and life? Do we believe that India will find these by recourse to the finer and nobler elements of her own ancient literature, by any sublimation of her own religions? Do we not believe that she needs the discipline, the inspiration, the enlightenment of which the Cross of CHRIST is symbol, and the Name of CHRIST is fountain?

What is wanted after all is simple. It is the witness of the things which have given England her best; faith in a Living GOD and FATHER; simple reverence for His likeness in the personality of every living soul; keen and clear conscience; a strong sense by the conscience' teaching of what evil is, what the conflict between evil and good, and what the victory of CHRIST; a loving, patient, invincible sympathy for all whom He has made. Any life which will come out from Oxford bearing that witness in faith and simplicity will be welcome, and will be of untold power in the coming days. There may be suffering, there may be disappointment, there may quite well—in some possible contingencies of the future—be personal danger; but there will be unfailing opportunity. But this is not the whole of what is asked of Oxford or of

what Oxford ought to give. In India, and in
Calcutta, there is a supreme call for her best. The
LORD could do His work by the Galilean fishermen,
but when the problem of mediating between the
Gospel and the Gentile world was to be met He
converted to Himself the highly-equipped Saul, and
made him the vessel of choice. I compare small
things perhaps with great, when I ask whether from
Oxford there cannot come out some of her best-
trained sons, trained to weigh and compare and
distinguish, with power of language to expound, and
power of thought to impress. This is the reinforce-
ment for which the gallent men at the front especially
look and pray. In this generation of supreme crisis
in the dealings of England, and England's Church,
with India, will Oxford stand dumb before that
appeal ?

EDW. SOUTHWARK.

THE PALACE, CALCUTTA.
    Feb. 7, 1910.

CONTENTS

CHAPTER I

PAGE

ORIGIN OF THE MISSION (1879–1885)   -   -   1

CHAPTER II

TROUBLED TIMES (1886–1889)   -   -   -   -   17

CHAPTER III

THE SCHOOLS AND THE SUNDERBANS   -   -   -   35

CHAPTER IV

THE NEW MISSION HOUSE   -   -   -   -   55

CHAPTER V

THE CALCUTTA UNIVERSITY   -   -   -   -   66

CHAPTER VI

THE INDUSTRIAL SCHOOL AND VISITS TO PATNA   -   92

CHAPTER VII

THE BARISAL MISSIONS   -   -   -   -   -   104

xxi

CHAPTER VIII

PAGE

ANNUS INFAUSTUS   -   -   -   -   -   -   126

CHAPTER IX

CONVERTS   -   -   -   -   -   -   -   -   142

CHAPTER X

1898–1908   -   -   -   -   -   -   -   -   155

CHAPTER XI

HINDUISM AS IT IS   -   -   -   -   -   -   183

APPENDIX

THE BRAHMO SOMAJ   -   -   -   -   -   -   213

INDEX -   -   -   -   -   -   -   -   -   219

LIST OF ILLUSTRATIONS

FACING PAGE

THE MOST REV. EDWARD RALPH JOHNSON, BISHOP OF
    CALCUTTA, 1876–98 - - - - *Frontispiece*

THE REV. E. F. WILLIS - - - - - - 4

FIRST HOUSE OF THE OXFORD MISSION IN BOW BAZAAR
    STREET, CALCUTTA - - - - - - 6

OXFORD MISSION HOUSE, MUKTARAM BABU STREET - 21

OXFORD MISSION HOUSE. THE FESTIVAL, JANUARY, 1890 36

MISSION SHALTI (CANAL BOAT) - - - - - 46

TWO MEN DRAINING WATER FROM A POND. SMALL
    BOYS CATCHING FISH WITH BASKETS - - - 49

FAMILY COOKING OUT OF DOORS IN THE COURTYARD OF
    A VILLAGE HOUSE IN THE SUNDERBANS - - 50

BAMBOO BRIDGE OVER A CANAL IN THE SUNDERBANS - 53

OXFORD MISSION HOUSE, CORNWALLIS STREET, CAL-
    CUTTA - - - - - - - - 57

LIDDON LECTURE ROOM FITTED AS CHAPEL FOR THE
    FESTIVAL - - - - - - - - 58

OXFORD MISSION CHAPEL, CALCUTTA - - - 60

COMMON ROOM, MISSION HOUSE, CALCUTTA - - 63

FIRST HOSTEL, CALCUTTA - - - - - 87

BHOOBAN MOHUN SIRCAR'S LANE - - - - 88

INDUSTRIAL SCHOOL BOYS AT WORK - - - 94

OXFORD MISSION SCHOOL VIOLIN CLASS - - - 97

BOATS ON THE RIVER NEAR BARISAL - - - - 106

FACING PAGE

WOMAN CARRYING WATERPOT AND CHILD - - - 117

THE RIGHT REV. HENRY WHITEHEAD, D.D., LORD
  BISHOP OF MADRAS - - - - - - 154

IN THE MISSION COMPOUND, BARISAL - - - 157

CHURCH AT BARISAL - - - - - - 158

MISSION SCHOOL BOYS, BARISAL - - - 160

BARISAL CHURCH INTERIOR - - - - 163

SOME OF THE SCHOOL BOYS AT BARISAL - - - 164

SISTERS' HOUSE, BARISAL - - - - - 166

NATIVE HUTS AT JOBARPAR. MEN MAKING A HUT
  WALL - - - - - - - 168

OXFORD MISSION HOSTEL, DACCA, 1908–1909 - - 171

DACCA HOSTEL - - - - - - - 172

GROUP OF MEMBERS OF THE MISSION, 1904 - - 174

SHILLONG—CHAPEL AND SISTERS' REST HOUSE BEYOND 181

SNAKE CHARMER AND COBRA - - - - 183

A SHORT HISTORY

OF THE

OXFORD MISSION TO CALCUTTA

᪥

CHAPTER I

ORIGIN OF THE MISSION

1879—1885

> " Men of action these !
> Who, seeing just as little as you please,
> Yet turn that little to account,—engage
> With, do not gaze at,—carry on, a stage,
> The work of the world, not merely make report."

IN the spring of 1879 one of the Cowley Fathers, who was holding a mission in Calcutta, was impressed with the great readiness which he found among the young educated Bengalis to discuss religious questions, and even to attend services at which he was able to preach to them. Many of them were members of the Brahmo Somaj,[1] a theistic sect of the Hindus, which at that time was attracting a good deal of attention in Calcutta;

[1] See Appendix, p. 213.

and there appeared to him to exist among them a strong sense of unsettlement and dissatisfaction with their own system of belief. This feeling and the evident religious susceptibilities of these young men seemed to him to offer a real opportunity for Christian missionary work among them. So strongly did Bishop Johnson, the Metropolitan, share this impression that he then and there wrote off to Oxford and entreated that an effort might be made, analogous to that of Cambridge in their hopeful Delhi Mission, to send out University men with the special object of working among the students of the University of Calcutta. Such was the origin of the Oxford Mission to Calcutta; and it must ever be a matter of deep thankfulness that it began its work in the Episcopate and under the encouragement of Bishop Johnson, whose wise and unfailing sympathy guided it through many difficulties, whose truly catholic mind was able to conceive a great idea of what such a Mission could do, and who watched over it with a most generous and ungrudging love.

It is worthy of note that the idea of the special character of the Mission—that of a Brotherhood living under a definite but simple rule of life—was largely due to an influence which came from India. Bishop Douglas, of Bombay, had, not long before, published his famous charge, urging the need of men and women organized in some form of the religious life for the work of Indian Missions. This charge had moved many in England very deeply; and when the idea of an Oxford Mission to

Calcutta took shape, it was determined that it should go as a community of men, bound indeed by no life vows, but united by devotion to a common work and obedience to a common rule of life, with the special aim of setting an example of regular Christian devotion by the maintenance of frequent common services. From the first, two main principles have been kept in view:

1. That the Mission should be free to develop its work as experience and circumstances might direct.

2. That the Members of the Mission should form a religious Brotherhood under a rule definite enough to give real strength and support to the spiritual life, and yet sufficiently elastic to enable the community to undertake work of very various kinds.

On these two principles the Mission has rested from the first, and experience has amply proved the wisdom of the course which has been adopted. There was one other influence at work, which was alluded to by Bishop King in a speech which he made at the annual meeting of the Oxford Mission in 1885. " I think," he said, " one of the strongest influences which urged this Mission forward was the intellectual pressure and trouble which were round about us at Oxford at that time, when men were comparing different kinds of religion, and almost feeling bound in freedom of thought to say, ' Let us look it fairly in the face. If these old Indian philosophic religions are better than we thought, let us be brave, let us admit the truth.' "

It was this intellectual pressure, this desire to investigate the great Indian religious systems, and to place them in their right relation to the Christian Faith, which the Bishop states were among the motives which led the first members of the Mission to offer themselves for the work.

The four graduates who formed the first members of the Oxford Mission were the Rev. Edward Francis Willis, M.A., of Balliol College, and Vice-Principal of Cuddesdon Theological College; the Rev. Ernest Faulkner Brown, M.A., scholar of Trinity College, and the Rev. Wilfrid Bird Hornby, M.A., of Brasenose College, both curates of S. Margaret's, Anfield, Liverpool; and the Rev. Marsham Frederick Argles, Fellow of S. John's College, and Principal of S. Stephen's House, Oxford. Of these, the first three, after a farewell service in the cathedral at Christ Church, at which the Bishop of Oxford gave them his benediction, sailed from Liverpool on October 30, 1880. With them went also a young layman, Edwin Berryman, who had been a page-boy at Cuddesdon, and now as a printer offered his services for a time to the Mission, to take charge of the printing-press which Mr. Willis took out with him. While he was with the Mission he proved himself a most valuable helper, especially at the time of Mr. Willis's illness, during which the entire management and responsibility of the work connected with the press rested upon him. Mr. Argles was unable to leave Oxford at this time, and it was arranged that he should join them in the October of the following year. They reached

The Rev. E. F. Willis.

[*To face p.* 4.

Calcutta on December 2nd, and received a very hearty welcome from the Bishop and from the clergy generally, as well as an address of welcome from the members of the Brahmo Somaj. A house had been provided for them by the Bishop in Bow Bazaar, a street which practically divides the English and the native portion of Calcutta, and which was within fairly easy access of both.

The Mission House was formally opened on the Festival of the Epiphany (January 6, 1881). There was a special benedictory service, followed by a Celebration of the Holy Eucharist, at which the Metropolitan was the celebrant, and at which the Rev. E. F. Willis, Rev. E. F. Brown, and Rev. W. B. Hornby were admitted members of the Oxford Brotherhood of S. Paul, and the Rev. E. F. Willis was installed as Superior. Thus, with the blessing of the Bishop, and with the sympathy and in the presence of a large number of clergy, the Mission began its work.

From the nature of the case this had to be at first somewhat tentative; the Mission had to feel its way, to see in what directions openings were offered, and to learn by experience the best methods of making use of them. The learning of Bengali took up, of course, at first, a good deal of their time; for, though it is true that nearly all the educated men speak English, yet it is obvious that a knowledge of the native language is of the greatest importance for gaining any real insight into the difficulties and needs of the students, while the circumstances of the Mission were sure to bring it into contact with a large number of non-English-speaking people. Lectures, individual interviews, and an occasional "At Home" were among the ways in which the Mission first began to get into touch with the educated Bengalis. A certain amount of printing, in the way of tracts and translations of books, was done by means of the printing-press. But the first permanent bit of work, curiously enough, sprang out of the relation of the Mission to the native Christians in Calcutta. These had for various reasons been left with very inadequate supervision, and it was evident from the first that any appeal to the non-Christians would be much weakened if those who were already baptized and belonged to the Church were presenting a very imperfect picture of Christian life. This the Bishop felt very strongly, and urged the Oxford Mission to undertake the charge of the native Christian congregation known as the "Cathedral Mission," and, by holding good native services and generally supervising the pastoral work among them, to raise the level of native Christian life. Though the native Christian congregations in Calcutta have always been in close touch with the Oxford Mission, and have received much help from it, yet they have not, with the exception of some brief periods, been actually under the charge of the Mission. But it was out of this connection that there grew the very important work of the establishment of a High School for the sons of native Christian parents.

The arrival of the Rev. M. F. Argles in December, 1881, made it easier to undertake this work ; and the

FIRST HOUSE OF THE OXFORD MISSION IN BOW BAZAAR STREET, CALCUTTA.

[To face p. 6.

school was opened early in 1882 as a boarding-school
for native Christian boys, with a view to educating
them up to the entrance examination of the Calcutta
University.   The fees charged were only ten rupees
a month; but even that proved too great an expense
for many of the parents, more especially the pastors,
whose sons it was particularly desired to attract.
Mr. Willis therefore made an appeal to friends at
home to form a scholarship fund to pay the fees of
deserving boys.   This appeal was cordially taken up,
and the fund so established has been maintained
ever since.

The opening of a school for native Christian boys
might seem at first sight somewhat of a departure
from the primary aim of the Mission—namely,
direct missionary work among the students; but the
members of the Mission, and others who had had
considerable experience of the mission-field in India,
all agreed that not only did the school not interfere
with missionary work, but was, on the contrary, a
very real help to it: and this for two reasons—first,
because a sound and thoroughly Christian education
would materially raise the standard of Christian
life in Calcutta; and, secondly, because the school
afforded the means of laying the foundation of one
of the greatest wants of the Church in India—a
well-trained native ministry.   There was not, it
must be remembered, at this time a single Christian
boarding-school for boys in Calcutta, and the want
of such a school was seen in the comparison of the
influence of native Christianity in Calcutta and in
South India.   A Hindu critic in Calcutta, who was

not unfriendly to the Christian religion, said that
"the native Christians raised no ripple on the
surface of Hindu society"; whereas in Southern
India, where scarcely any Mission is without its
boarding-school for boys and girls, it is the evidence
of the Hindus themselves that the native Christians,
belonging for the most part to low castes, are winning their way to a leading position in the community, equal, if not superior, to that of the Brah-
mans.

Thus, at the end of 1882, in rather less than two
years after the arrival of the first brethren, the work
of the Mission was beginning to assume definite
shape, and the Superior and his fellow-workers were
beginning to see something of the lines on which
they might hope to develop the work in the future,
and were already turning their minds to the question of permanent and enlarged buildings. In fact,
the growth of the school necessitated the hiring of
another house close by that which was occupied
by the Mission, the rent of which the Bishop of
Calcutta still continued very generously to pay.

All that had hitherto been done with regard
to the constitution of the Brotherhood had been
provisional. But the experience of two years had
shown that the rule and constitution had worked
satisfactorily; and it was therefore with a good hope
and glad heart that the community was formally
constituted by the Bishop on the Festival of the
Epiphany, 1883. Only one change was made, and
that was in respect of the name, which was altered
from that of S. Paul to that of the Epiphany—

a name which, for obvious reasons, seemed especially appropriate; and from this date the Mission has been known as the Brotherhood of the Epiphany.

But the year which had begun so hopefully was soon to bring a heavy cloud over the Mission. Mr. Argles had scarcely been twelve months in Calcutta when his health gave way, and he was ordered home. He died within a fortnight of his arrival in England. His loss was a very heavy one.

Mr. Gore,[1] writing of his death, said:

" The Church of England, from the point of view of her own apparent needs, has reason to deplore deeply the untimely loss of the Rev. Marsham Frederick Argles. We have not too many men who combine with intelligence and ability an unwavering and persistent strength of conviction and purpose. The words from the Lesson in the Burial Office, ' stedfast, unmoveable always abounding in the work of the LORD,' are the best description of his character. He was pre-eminently simple, gentle, truthful, and at all times rigorously obedient to conscience. In faith and practice wholly Catholic, he seemed to give himself, specially among Christian duties, to the cultivation of prayer and fasting. Wherever he was, he was for ever diffusing around him an atmosphere of steadiness, patience, and happiness; he was intolerant of nothing but sin and indolence or unhopefulness in Christians. He was full of an affection, strong and deep rather than demonstrative. Such he was, and so he grew without check from his first coming up to Oxford;

[1] Now the Bishop of Birmingham (1909).

and so there was steadily developed and matured
in him that temper of cheerful discipline which
made a ' religious ' life seem natural to him, and
that vocation to missionary work, the first consciousness of which dated from his boyhood. To
this vocation he responded so loyally that it would
have been, as he said just before he left England,
a greater self-denial to him to stay at home than
to go to India ; and to it he finally sacrificed his
life. His friends would agree that they have never
known a character which it is more easy to think
of in the tranquil waiting state of Paradise."

Hardly had this blow fallen, coming as it did so
unexpectedly, than the Mission received another.
In the summer of the same year the health of the
Superior broke down. He, too, had to return home,
and, though he lived fifteen years longer, his illness
was such that he was unable to return to India,
and, indeed, he was incapacitated for further work
of any kind. It was the old story, the story of
overwork ; of one who, with untiring energy and
ceaseless enthusiasm, overrated his physical strength
and simply wore himself out. He died in England,
May 12, 1898.

Writing shortly after his death, Bishop Hornby[1]
said :

" At this moment it almost startles me to think
of that marvellous capacity for work, that ceaseless
activity, until the delicate machinery of the mind

[1] The Rev. Wilfrid Bird Hornby became Bishop of Nyasaland in 1892, and is now (1909) Bishop of Nassau in the
Bahama Islands.

at last gave way. Let me think of some of the
occupations of his *daily* life in the short two and
a half years that limited his period of work. The
management of a large Indian household, every
detail of which was submitted to himself; the
preparation of lectures to educated Hindus; the
preaching to European or native congregations;
the learning of the Bengali language, in which he
was able to preach more or less intelligibly at
the end of a year—and *that* a language which
the Bengalis themselves would not allow that
any European had really mastered. Then came
the daily superintendence of the boys' boarding-school, some thirty little boys, children of
Bengali Christian parents. To all this were
added the ceaseless interruptions — visits from
native Christian gentlemen, visits from native
students at the University of Calcutta, and, as if
this were not enough, the editing of the *Indian
Churchman* and superintendence of the printing-
press—which employed some sixteen native printers,
with an English boy called Berryman as acting
sub-manager—and the revising of all proofs, which
he did himself.

"As one looks back to the early years of the
Oxford Mission life in Calcutta, one concludes that
Willis was unfitted by the very variety of his own
attainments to be the Superior of a great under-
taking. He would have done better work himself,
and better work would have been got out of the
other members of the Mission, if we had been
under the control of a man who had a truer

understanding of the limits of human endurance
in a climate like Calcutta, where for three months
of the year the thermometer stands at 102 degrees
in the shade. But, wherever his weakness lay,
Willis set to all Cuddesdon men a noble example
of what can be done in a short time ; possibly,
too, of what can *not* be done—for the bow was
stretched till at last it broke."

The loss of Mr. Willis and of Mr. Argles would
have been serious at any time; they were specially
so when the Mission was, as it were, still in its
childhood, and when the development of the work
required an increasing and not a diminishing staff.
One great encouragement had been the arrival of
the Rev. Philip Samuel Smith, Fellow of S. Augustine's College, Canterbury, and late scholar of University College, Oxford.

But even with the accession of Mr. Smith the
Mission was very much undermanned, and it was
therefore with a real sense of thankfulness that they
received the news that the Rev. Charles Gore, who
had succeeded Mr. Willis as Vice-Principal of
Cuddesdon, had offered to spend the first nine
months of 1894 with the Mission in Calcutta. He
arrived in January, accompanied by Mr. Peach, who
also came as a visitor. Another event which took
place in this year, and which was eventually to have
the greatest influence on the work of the Mission,
was the appointment of the Rev. Henry Whitehead,[1]
Fellow of Trinity College, Oxford, to the post of
Principal of Bishop's College, Calcutta.

[1] Consecrated Bishop of Madras, June, 1899.

Meantime the general work of the Mission had been maintained. The school continued to increase, and in April, 1883, had reached a total of twenty-five. Lectures, interviews, and visits kept up and widened the influence of the Mission among the students and educated Bengalis; and a good deal of intercourse took place at this time between the members of the Mission and the Brahmo Somaj, whose leader was Keshub Chunder Sen. But perhaps one of the most important developments of the work in this year was the starting of the *Epiphany*—a weekly paper, edited by the members of the Mission, for the discussion of religious, literary, and social topics, and written specially for the university students. It was in the days when the Mission was feeling most keenly the loss of Mr. Willis and Mr. Argles, that Mr. Smith, with characteristic hopefulness, suggested the starting of something new, and the *Epiphany* was the result. It has been carried on continuously since its first publication, and has proved an instrument of increasing usefulness. It has obtained a recognized place in Calcutta, and is frequently referred to by the native press; while by means of the "Answers to inquirers" which it gives, it affords an opportunity for spreading an immense amount of information about Christianity, and, what is not less important, for correcting a still greater amount of misconception. It was at first published at the nominal price of a farthing, but has since been made free, and has now a circulation of about five thousand[1] copies a week. As most

[1] Ten thousand (1909).

of the copies are each read by two or three people at least, this means that the paper is read every week by about ten or twelve thousand non-Christians. Nor is its influence confined to Calcutta; it goes to many other parts of India, as well as to Burma and Ceylon, and the Mission is constantly receiving testimonies from various sources as to its usefulness for missionary work.

But perhaps the most striking testimony to its influence was an article published last year (1898) in *The Statesman*, one of the leading daily papers in Calcutta. "The correspondence columns of the *Epiphany*," says the writer, "from week to week reveal all manner of religious speculation, of anxious inquiry, of bewildered thought. Some may regard it as too large a pretension for that journal to undertake to 'answer all questions respecting religion'; but doubtless the limitation is implied—to the extent of the light afforded by the Christian revelation. However that may be, it is impossible not to admire the fearlessness with which objections are met and the most difficult problems faced. Whether one can always agree with the Editor or not, it is undeniable that he burkes nothing. And amid a perfect babel of voices, which the correspondence columns echo, often involving questions which are silly or impertinent, the editor preserves unfailing tact and courtesy; his patience is unwearied, and he presents an example of the Christian spirit which the missionary body as a whole might well emulate in dealing with the youth of India. Of course the *Epiphany* is in touch with the modern scientific spirit of inquiry, and abreast of the historical problems which start up everywhere in connection with the old religions and the new forms of defence put forth on behalf of Hinduism and Buddhism. The Oxford Brothers are well versed in Hindu literature and philosophy, and not appalled by the Buddhist remains so diligently raked up everywhere. Every missionary society, we believe, has desired, at different times and in divers ways, to meet the religious wants of the educated youth of India, and has attempted to do so with more or less result. But the conspicuous success of the Oxford Mission in this respect is evidenced by the regular appearance of the *Epiphany*—which has now reached its fifteenth year of publication—and by the unfailing interest which English-speaking natives take in it, as its columns clearly show."

The year 1884 was one of considerable anxiety, but some idea as to the effect the Mission was already producing is shown by the following extract from a letter written by Mr. Gore after his arrival in Calcutta:

" I have been," he says, " a good deal impressed with manifold testimonies to the value of their work, specially the great work of edification among the native Christians. ' They have put a new spirit in us,' they say. They are deeply impressed with their simple love, their utter absence of superiority, and their genuine brotherliness. They have wonderfully prepared the way for Whitehead at Bishop's College; and you would have gone into ecstasies over a guild of native Christians that I talked to this morning at

the college.   Then they have done excellent good
work in opening out towards the native Babus : they
feel them such friends.   This is over and above the
actual conversions they have helped in.   This latter
work has been mainly that of Argles and Philip
Smith.   Brown is full of courage, zeal, and love.
The native Christians talk much about Hornby.   So
far, then, there is a wonderful deal to encourage.   It
would be the joy of my heart to stay, in a way.   We
must get some men.   It wants love much more than
great ability.   There is splendid work for anybody
who will come."

But the strain of the past year had been a heavy
one, and the Oxford Committee, in their annual
report, expressed their great thankfulness to
Mr. Brown and Mr. Smith for the unflinching
courage and devotion with which they have carried
on the work.   A further encouragement came in the
arrival of the Rev. Charles William Townsend, of
Keble College, Oxford, and Vice-Principal of
Salisbury Theological College ; and the Rev. Charles
Henley Walker, of Oriel College, Oxford, and
Curate of Dorchester, Oxon, who had offered themselves for the work of the Mission.   They had left
England in October, and reached Calcutta on
November 14, 1885, where they received a very
warm and hearty welcome, the boys of the school
especially decorating the house for the occasion.

CHAPTER II

TROUBLED TIMES

1886—1889

" One of the chief lessons of my life has been, that what seems most hindering is most helpful."

WITH the year 1886 began what may be termed the second period of the work of the Mission. This was marked in Calcutta by the removal of the centre of the Mission from Bow Bazaar to the more immediate neighbourhood of the students' quarter of the city; and at home by the appointment of Miss Murray as General Secretary, a work at the service of which she placed, for the next ten years, her unrivalled energy and self-devotion. It is to her more than any one that the Mission owes the large and enthusiastic organization at home, without which means could not, humanly speaking, have been found for supporting and extending the work in Calcutta, which was soon to grow so largely. To a zeal which never tired Miss Murray added a hope and faith which knew no discouragement; and it is not too much to say that to her, more than to any one, except perhaps the Bishop of Lincoln, Mr. Whitehead, and Mr. Brown, does the Mission owe the position and prosperity which it has to-day.

Mr. Townsend was installed as Superior on the Festival of the Epiphany by the Bishop of Calcutta, and the next few months were mainly occupied with the negotiations for a new house. For some time it had been felt that the house in Bow Bazaar was practically too far from where the students lived to enable the Mission to have that close touch with them which they desired, and they had consequently been hoping for an opportunity of getting a house nearer to the students' quarter, which lies, roughly speaking, within the square formed by Machooa Bazaar Street, Amherst Street, Beadon Street, and Chitpore Road.

Hitherto, one difficulty with regard to the move had been the High School. This could not well be left at Bow Bazaar, and it was impossible to find a suitable house with a playground in the native quarter of the city. But just at this time the Society for the Propagation of the Gospel offered to build a house in the compound at Bishop's College, and to allow the Mission to use it for its school. The school-house remained the property of the Society, the head master and the expenses of the school being provided by the Mission. Mr. Brown, whose child the school had practically been from the first, continued in charge when they moved into their new home. In the *Quarterly Paper* of the Mission he gives an account of the ordinary routine of the school:

"We begin the day at the High School with Prime at six, in Bengali, after which the boys go to preparation till half-past eight, and then, after a short interval, they have breakfast. Their dining-room is not very luxurious or æsthetic. It is a detached building, consisting of one hall, about thirty feet by ten, quite innocent of furniture—for the boys do not eat sitting on chairs and at tables; they simply sit on strips of matting which are laid on the floor, and eat with their plates on the ground before them. After breakfast comes a short interval, and then they go into school at ten minutes past ten, and in school they stay till four, except for an interval of one hour, from one to two. At four we have Bengali Evensong for the smaller boys in the college chapel, together with the boys of the S.P.G. Boarding School. This is followed at half-past four by English Evensong for the college students and the elder boys of the school. Then comes foot-ball, or gymnastics, till half-past six, when they dine. After dinner they have preparation till Compline at a quarter to nine, and then bed. The little boys go to bed at eight. We have fixed days for foot-ball—Mondays Thursdays, and Saturdays—when all boys must turn out, unless disabled. On Tuesdays and Fridays they get lessons in gymnastics for a part of the evening. The boys have lately developed a fondness for tennis, and, indeed, some of them have made considerable progress in the game.

"As to holidays, we have the usual vacations every year, and we have half-holidays on all saints' days and Saturdays, when we close work at one, and have no preparation at night. On Sundays the boys attend an English service in the college chapel, and a Bengali one in the cathedral in the

morning; i.e., they go to Holy Communion and
Mattins every Sunday in the chapel and cathedral
alternately. On Sunday afternoons they attend
Bengali Evensong at the cathedral at four. Besides
these services, the elder boys go to the celebration
of the Holy Eucharist on saints' days in the college
chapel, and we have Bengali Mattins for all afterwards at ten: on these days and on Sundays Prime
is not said.

"This is the picture of the regular routine of
the school. Of course now and then we have
little incidents which emerge from the ordinary
monotonous round; such a one has just taken place,
namely the holding of the University examination, in
which we take a great interest this year, for we have
sent in two boys for the entrance or matriculation
examination. The boys themselves are confident
of their success; the teachers entertain doubts.
Let us hope that the scholars may prove the more
competent judges of their own cases. After matri-
culating from the school, a boy, if he wishes to
continue his studies, would probably go on to
Bishop's College. We gave the college two boys
last year, and will probably give them these two if
they get through their examination."

Of the value of the school Mr. Townsend wrote
soon after his arrival, "I am fully convinced that
it is among the most solid work that the Mission
is doing"; and the Bishop, who still continued his
munificent contributions to the funds of the Mission,
was equally warm in his praise of the influence
which the school was exerting.

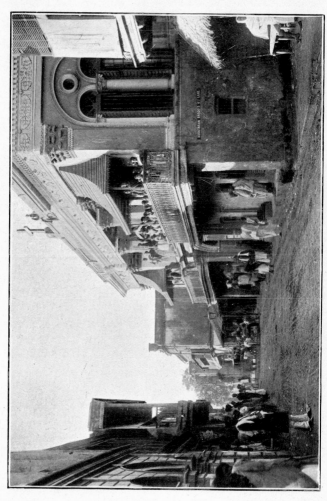

OXFORD MISSION HOUSE, MUKTARAM BABU STREET.

Two benefactions have been given to the school, one by some Bengali friends of Mr. Argles, who presented to the Mission, through Mr. M. L. Sandel, the sum of one hundred and thirty rupees to found an "Argles memorial prize"; and the other was received in 1888, when, on the retirement of Archdeacon Atlay, his numerous friends in Calcutta, desirous to preserve some memorial of him, subscribed a sum of four thousand three hundred rupees for that purpose; and he, with the generosity which always characterized him, desired that the memorial should be nothing personal, but should form a fund for maintaining a scholar at the High School.

Having thus provided for the school, the Mission was free to move as soon as a house could be found. The one finally decided upon was at 99 Muktaram Babu Street, which, as to situation and size, seemed to be fairly suitable. The formal entry into the new quarters was made early on the morning of June 17, 1886, when the clergy and choir went round the house in procession; prayers were said in the principal rooms, and the first Holy Eucharist was offered, in Bengali, in the chapel.

The house was the ordinary house of a well-to-do Hindu gentleman, built round two quadrangles, the inner one of which had been used as the Zenana or ladies' part of the house. Though covering a good deal of ground and containing a large number of rooms, the rooms themselves were small and low, conditions which made them trying for a European to live in. The one large central room was used for the chapel, and made as bright and devotional

as possible by means of the gifts of many kind
friends. The neighbourhood was of course very
different from that of Bow Bazaar, being entirely
in the native part of the city, where the dirt, the
smells, and the noise of native life make life for the
European very trying, not only during the day,
but often at night as well.

"Our street," writes a member of the Mission "is
an odd jumble of squalor and splendour. There
are two towering mansions just opposite us, inhabited by some very wealthy Babus and their
joint families, all living together in the Indian style.
The garden in front of the larger is decorated with
ridiculous stucco statues in the Greek style, and is
full of cranes, emus, and other queer bipeds. On
two sides our Mission House is surrounded with
'Busti,' or native huts—mud and straw shanties
roofed with tiles. One is directly under my bed-
room; and the family who inhabit it are rather
amusing, especially when they have 'jars,' which
is not unfrequently. To hear a Bengali woman
vociferate in voluble Billingsgate, at about one
hundred words in a breath is astonishing. Occasionally they are 'at home with music,' which is
rather trying, as they keep it up till long after
midnight. The instrumental part is of the tom-tom
order, and the vocal very nasal, with long shakes.
The songs are generally religious—hymns to Rama
and Krishna. One likes it for a little, but it is
apt to get monotonous."

The central event of 1887, and one which brought
a heavy sorrow and loss upon the Mission, was the

death of Mr. Philip Smith. Never very strong, he knew when he offered himself for the work of the Mission that he had not many years to live ; but, as he characteristically said, India was as good a country to die in as any other. Once at Calcutta he never spared himself, but threw his whole energy and soul into the work before him, devoting himself with a special zeal, and with a unique power, to the service of the University students, and, by his sympathy, self-devotion, and love for them, winning in the short space of little more than three years a wonderful position among them. Nor was it the students alone who felt the influence of his character. Every one who came in contact with him was drawn towards him ; and the large and reverent crowd which attended his funeral, composed of English and Bengalis, Christians and non-Christians, of all shades of opinion, testified to the regard in which he was held. When the present writer was in Calcutta in 1893 his name was still remembered among the students with affection and respect. It was largely with money lent by Mr. Smith that the house in Muktaram Babu Street was bought, and in accordance with his expressed desire his brother at his death made over the property to the Mission. But perhaps a still greater gift was his grave, which, as Mr. Townsend wrote, is an abiding pledge of the continuance of the work of the Mission.

Of the many tributes which were paid to Mr. Smith's work, none was more true or happy than that of Sir William Hunter, K.C.S.I., Vice-Chancellor

of the Calcutta University, who spoke of what
Mr. Smith's life and influence had been, at the
annual meeting of the Mission, at Oxford, in May,
1888:

"I should like here to say a few words about
one of the Oxford Brethren lately deceased. Some
of you here knew Philip Smith. He was a man,
although he died at thirty-three, whose influence will
last for many years. Many of his friends have
regretted his early decease. But if you adopt the
principle which he adopted, the principle of renunciation of this world, you will rather rejoice in a
death which carried out the purpose for which he
lived. There has been no event in the history of
the Mission which so powerfully impressed the native
mind as the calm ending of this one young Oxford
scholar, who gave up his life to his duty. If you
will allow me, I should like to read a few comments
made at the time of his death by native newspapers
—newspapers written and edited by non-Christians
of various Indian beliefs. One of them says: 'We
knew him not only as a preacher of Christianity,
but also as a fellow-worker in every noble cause
calculated to uplift the people. To our young men
he was a friend and counsellor in all their needs.'
Another of them, the editor of a Bengali political
paper, writes: 'His courtesy to all men, high and
low, his attention to boys and children, his sympathy
with the distressed, his active charity, will be
remembered by all who knew him.'

"The following sentences, which are translated
from a journal written in the Bengali language, bear

a still stronger testimony to his worth: ' Uncom-
promising Christian though he was, he mixed freely
with all sorts of people, conversed with them on
religious topics, whatever might be their colour or
their creed. Crowds of ragged and dirty boys
would gather round him in the streets, and pull
his clothes or plague him in other ways, but he
would kindly take them up and kiss them.' Now
think what this means. A white man walks through
the Calcutta streets, a scholar and a gentleman,
and poor boys of different religion and race have
such confidence in him that they press round him
and cling to the skirts of his garment, and ask
him to kiss them. Is there not a similar picture
handed down from old times? Philip Smith really
made the Hindus in Calcutta understand that the
old narrative was a true narrative, and that Christianity is as living to-day as it was in Palestine
eighteen centuries ago."

As some compensation for this heavy loss, the
year 1888 brought a welcome accession to the staff
of the Mission, in the person of the Rev. Maurice
Bell, of Hertford College, Oxford, who reached
Calcutta on the eve of the festival of the Epiphany,
thus adding an extra element of gladness to what is
always a day of great happiness to the Mission.
Unfortunately, a few months showed that the climate
of Calcutta was hopeless for Mr. Bell, and to his
own and the Brethren's great regret he was ordered
by the doctor to return to England.

Two other priests had meanwhile offered themselves to the Mission: the Rev. James Legard Peach

E

of Trinity College, Cambridge, who, it will be remembered, had, while a layman, come out as a visitor to Calcutta with Mr. Gore in 1884; and the Rev. Halhed Sydney Moore, of Keble College, Oxford, curate to Mr. Hornby, Vicar of S. Columba, Sunderland, one of the first members of the Mission. They both arrived in November, 1888.

Of the daily life at the Mission House at this time the following account, written by Mr. Brown in 1889, gives a very good idea; and we may add that in its main features it represents the ordinary daily life of the Mission as it is to-day:

"One day is indeed very like another at the Mission House, and to describe an average day will be to set before you a very large part of our life. Well, then, the day begins with Prime at six; and in the tropics the variation between the hours of sunrise and of sunset in different parts of the year is so small that we find it most convenient to keep to the same time-table all the year round. Prime is followed by the Holy Communion (daily), and most days of the week one of us goes to celebrate for the Sisters at the Canning Home. This is followed by that cup of tea which goes by the name of *chota hazari*, 'the little breakfast,' which is so essential to one's life that without it we are flabby, nerveless organisms, useless for any task either spiritual or bodily. It is humiliating to be such a victim to external conditions; but, though I think I may count myself as strong as most Anglo-Indians, I can never forego my *chota hazari* without paying for the omission by a headache for the rest of the

day. Meditation, Mattins, and Terce then occupy
us till breakfast, at 9.30. At breakfast a book is
read; and as a general rule during the earlier part
of the day, till Sext, silence is observed, except in
so far as our work requires it to be broken. After
breakfast there are household duties to be attended
to and letters to be answered. One has to go to
teach at the school of the Society for the Propagation of the Gospel at Howrah, another probably
to visit the school for poor boys which a Hindu
Pundit has established in our lecture-room. Our
Rule requires an hour's study of the Bible every
day; and if after this has been done there is any
part of the morning remaining, it is devoted to
private reading or to Bengali lessons. Sext is said
at twelve. Tiffin is at one, a book being read as
at breakfast. The interval till None, at 2.45, is
a time of recreation, and is spent in talk, reading
the papers, and possibly (if it be very hot) in a
little gentle and refreshing slumber.

"After None the Babus begin to come. The
house is open to them at all times; but they consult
both their own convenience and ours by coming
in the afternoon and evening. They are mostly of
the student class, or are young clerks in offices;
but here and there a grey head may be seen
amongst them. Most afternoons there is a pretty
constant stream of them coming in to use the
reading-room, to borrow books, to talk, or to 'read
Bible,' as they express it; and our aim is to draft
them off to our own rooms by ones or twos—seldom
more at a time—and then learn from them their

thoughts, their difficultes, their doubts; to teach
them the great truths of the Faith, and to press
home to their consciences those moral and spiritual
facts which they are generally willing enough to
recognize intellectually. This is our main work;
and we look upon all our classes, lectures, debates,
'at homes,' and Mission Services—into all of which
we launch out occasionally—as leading up to this.
One would think that one or two such interviews,
when one gets a man face to face, and can speak
to him heart to heart and soul to soul, would make
a great impression; but that is just where the
difference comes in between a Bengali and an
Englishman. An Englishman will not readily open
his mouth on a religious subject, but if he does he
means it. The Bengali is always ready to talk
about religion—nothing is easier than to get him
on to a religious subject; but then one discovers,
to one's great disappointment, that his interest in
it is merely intellectual and superficial, and that
nothing is further from his thoughts than to accept
any responsibility for such truth as he is led to
acknowledge. There are those that have gone on
visiting us actually from the time when the Mission
was first started, and yet it would be hard to affirm
that they had made the smallest progress towards
the truth. However, the usual course is for these
to drop off after a time. Of course there are others
who make real advance; some whose consciences
are aroused, whose hearts are touched, and who
emerge at last from the stage of inquirers into that
of catechumens. There are more, in whom the seed

has really taken root, but its fruit will not be visible for many years. There have been several instances lately in Calcutta of old men being baptized whose knowledge of Christianity began in their boyhood. There are more still who will never come to Holy Baptism at all, but whose lives will have been elevated by what they have learnt at the Mission House, and who will help to secure that recognition of duty and conscience which more than anything else is required as the *Præparatio Evangelica* in India.

" Our Babus generally depart to their own evening meal as it grows dark, and we then have Evensong and dinner. After dinner there is often some meeting, which it is useful to attend ; otherwise we go to bask in the air, which by this time has begun to blow cool, upon the roof—'to eat the wind,' according to the expressive Bengali idiom. Compline is at nine, and after it we generally find our way pretty quickly to bed. The great difficulty in India is to do an honest day's work, for without having done very much I have often in the hot weather found myself so tired by night-time that I could not take the trouble to wind up my watch."

Outside the Mission House the Brethren occasionally preached in one of the many squares which were in the neighbourhood. That outdoor preaching was not a method they very often used was not from any disparagement of that form of missionary work, for if rightly done it cannot be too highly spoken of. But Calcutta was well supplied with bazaar preachers; and the members of the Mission felt that the more individual work of lectures and interviews, of which they had as much as they could manage, was the special kind of work for which they were best fitted.

Another method of contact with the students, and one to which at this time the Mission devoted a good deal of attention, was attending, either as visitor or president, some of the various clubs, in the formation of which the Calcutta student seems to take so much delight. They are established in great numbers and for various purposes, mostly literary, moral, or religious.

Such a club was the " Home Club," which met once a week to read the Bible and discuss religious subjects. They invited Mr. Smith to preside at their meetings, and after his death one or other of the members of the Mission went in his stead. Another was named the " Society for the study of CHRIST," and was formed by some of the members of a much larger club, known as the " Concord Club," but was entirely independent of it. The Mission also organized a debating club, with the aim of discussing social and literary problems in a healthy moral atmosphere, and thus influencing for good the minds of those who might attend the debates. It reached one hundred and forty members, and had Sir W. W. Hunter as its patron.

But the clubs were chiefly useful as a means of contact with the students, and of getting to know them with a view to closer personal intercourse. It is here that the real work is mostly done, and here too that the difficulty of the work mainly lies. For the Western and Eastern minds are widely

different. For many centuries they have been
moving in different directions, until time seems to
have raised an inexplicable barrier between them.
Pantheism, which for ages has been the prevailing
influence under which successive generations of
Hindus have lived, has coloured every mental movement, has stamped itself deep upon their religious
conviction, has dominated and affected almost every
department of their daily life. We are apt to consider Pantheism as an extinct philosophy, revived
in a modified form from time to time in some few
European minds; and it is well to remember that
in India it is a living thing, the influence under
which more than two hundred millions of men and
women to-day direct their religious, mental, and
social life.

We have spoken of it as a living thing, but a
"dead thing" would be a truer phrase. Whatever
attraction Pantheism may have to a mind which
accepts it in a society permeated and dominated by
Christianity, it is a very different thing when seen
in its effects in a society wholly under its influence.
Death and not life, the darkening and not the enlight-
ening of the human conscience, the enslavement not
the freedom of the human mind and will, are the
unmistakable results. In the deep-rooted Pantheism
of the Hindu, and the issues which it involves, lies
one of the great difficulties of missionary work in
India.[1] Wholly inconceivable to a Western mind
is such a statement as the following, which was

[1] Some more detailed account of what modern Hinduism
practically is will be found in the last chapter of this book.

made in all seriousness by an educated Hindu. At a religious discussion at the Mission House on the "Life and Resurrection of our LORD," a distinguished member of the University of Oxford, who was staying with the Mission, had stated the arguments for believing that JESUS CHRIST was a real person, with a clearness and power of logic which seemed incontrovertible. A Hindu gentleman who was present rose at the close of the address, and said, "It is not of the least consequence to me whether JESUS CHRIST was a real person or not. So long as I have the vision of the moral beauty which He sets before me, I do not care whether He lived or not."

But beyond and behind this difficulty of mental attitude lies another and a deeper one—one which is above all else the result of Pantheism—namely, that absence of the deep moral sense which we know as *conscience*, and which in some form or other asserts itself in every European. A man within the sphere of Christendom may be ignorant of religion, ignorant even of Christianity, he may be sunk in every kind of degradation and vice—yet deep down in his soul there is a clear and strong conviction of the difference between right and wrong. But this is very weak and sadly confused in the Hindu. The work, then, which the Mission has to do is largely the work of re-creating the moral sense, of recovering the idea of conscience, which for centuries has been buried beneath the deadening mass of Pantheism. This must be a slow work and an individual work; and though converts have from time to time been baptized, the Mission has never been disheartened because they have as yet been few.

In the spring of 1889 Mr. Brown started for a visit to England, after nine years of continuous and anxious work. This necessitated Mr. Peach taking up his residence at the High School, of which he took over the charge during Mr. Brown's absence; while Mr. Whitehead, who wished to bring Bishop's College into closer touch with the Mission, had asked that Mr. Walker might be lent to the college for a time to lecture to the students. This left practically only two resident members at the Mission House, the Superior (Mr. Townsend), and Mr. Moore.

It was soon after these arrangements were completed, and when the Mission seemed to be looking forward to a year of quiet and steady work, that a blow, heavier than any it had received before, fell upon it. Mr. Townsend felt obliged to make his submission to the Church of Rome. As far as he could, he did everything which was possible to minimize the result of his action upon the Mission ; but such a step on the part of the Superior could not fail to lay the Mission open to the charge that its teaching encouraged disloyalty to the English Church. Yet what appeared to be at the moment a grave disaster was turned into a victory by the courage and hopefulness, as well as by the unfaltering charity and faith, of those who remained. "As far as the band left without its head is concerned," wrote the Bishop, "all are brave, and feel that it is only a call to more devoted work."

F

That the step which Mr. Townsend felt himself compelled to take was in no way the outcome of the teaching of the Oxford Mission was fully proved by Mr. Brown in the following statement, which he made at the annual festival of the Mission in 1890, and for which he had Mr. Townsend's own authority :

" In leaving the English Church he (Mr. Townsend) adopted an entirely new principle. It has often been said, and it will often be said again, that the principles of the Oxford Mission lead to Rome. I can only say Townsend himself did not think so. He gave up the Anglican principle of the preservation of truth, and took in its stead the Roman principle of the development of truth. The one principle did not grow out of the other; it was a new plant from a new root. The one had to be uprooted before the other could take its place; and he went so far as to say, in the last conversation I had with him here, that he thought it would in some respects have been easier for him to reach his present conclusions if he had been brought up on a different system altogether—if he had been brought up, for instance, in the strictest Calvinism."

It was thus, then, that the crisis was met; and because it was thus met it was soon seen that what might, humanly speaking, have thrown back and largely wrecked the work, only left the Mission with stronger grounds of sober hope, with wider views for the future, and with more quiet confidence as to its place and course in the life of India, than perhaps at any previous time of its career.

CHAPTER III

The Schools and the Sunderbans

> " All the place
> Seemed less a cultivation than a waste.
> Men work here only, scarce begin to live."

THE record of the year we have now reached shows that the hope with which the Mission met the troubles of 1889 was not an unfounded one. If that year seemed at the moment to threaten a check, it was soon apparent that it was in reality only a period of preparation for a large extension of the work of the Mission in many directions.

On New Year's Day, 1890, the Rev. Walter Field, of Keble College, and S. John's, Kennington, arrived in Calcutta. Mr. Brown had returned a few weeks before, and during the last months of 1889 Mr. Lloyd, a layman, had come to work with Mr. White-head at Bishop's College. Mr. Lloyd did not actually join the Mission till some years later; but as an associate he took an active share in much of its work, and by his ability and gentleness, his insight into native character, and his great sympathy, became one of the most valuable and helpful supporters of the work.

The New Year, then, saw the Mission with its forces re-collected and reinforced, and what was a still greater fact, with a new Superior. It had been an open secret for some time that Mr. Whitehead had originally intended to offer himself for work with the Oxford Mission, but for the time the call to the management of Bishop's College appeared to be one which could not be put aside. As so often happens, what seemed at first a hindrance to his hopes was in the end the means to their fuller realization. For when the proposal was made that he should become Superior of the Oxford Mission, the Society for the Propagation of the Gospel raised no objection to his retaining the post of Principal of the College as well. And thus, without being united by any formal act, the works which had grown up round the Oxford Mission, and those which belonged to the Society for the Propagation of the Gospel in Calcutta and the immediate neighbourhood, became closely connected, and were directed practically by one head.

As Mr. Whitehead had long had the confidence of the members of the Mission, it was with a deep sense of thankfulness and joy that they welcomed him as their leader. But in accordance with the constitution he could not formally join the Brotherhood of the Epiphany until after a year's probation, so that the appointment had for the present to be provisional, the public and final installation being deferred till the Epiphany of 1891.

Another event which made the festival of 1890 noteworthy was the presence of Mr. Gore, who again visited the Mission, this time accompanied by Mr. Wakeman, Fellow of All Souls College,

OXFORD MISSION HOUSE. THE FESTIVAL, JANUARY, 1890.

[To face p. 36.

Oxford, and Treasurer of the Mission.[1] This second
visit was much shorter than the first, but coming,
as it did, after a period of such great anxiety, was
doubly welcome, and the Brethren had the additional
help of Mr. Gore as the conductor of their annual
Retreat.

It is now time to turn more especially to the
work of the Mission, which, as we have said, began
to show signs of expansion in various directions,
and which, from this date, begins to be more intimately connected with the various works belonging
to Bishop's College.

The Mission had been now for four years in
Muktaram Babu Street; and although the position
was a better one for the purposes of the work
than Bow Bazaar, the street in which it was situated
presented many drawbacks: and the house itself
proved far from convenient, owing to the smallness
of the rooms. The one big room being used for
the chapel, there was no other of sufficient size for
lectures or any large gatherings, for which purposes
a room had to be awkwardly extemporized in a
kind of back garden. No ground was to be had
adjoining the house for building; and though in the
quarter where the students lived, it was not in a
position readily seen, and therefore not as much
en évidence as was desirable. It seemed well, then,
to try to make another move, and it was resolved

---

[1] On the death of Dr. Wilson, late Warden of Keble, in
1897, Mr. Wakeman accepted the office of Vice-Chairman of
the Committee at home. His sudden death in the year 1900
was a very heavy loss to the Mission, which from the first
received his most generous and ungrudging support.

this time to build a house especially for the Mission. The idea was taken up eagerly by the committee at home; and the indefatigable secretary, Miss Murray, undismayed with having £3,000 to raise for an endowment fund for the school, set to work and with incredible rapidity collected the necessary funds for the new building.

The choice and acquisition of a site was a more lengthy and difficult task. One in every way suitable was at last found by Mr. Peach, facing Cornwallis Street, the main central thoroughfare of Calcutta, and the house was ready for use about the middle of 1891.

The first happy result of the closer connection between the Mission and Bishop's College was seen in the improved organization of the two schools connected with the college. Besides the High School, which belonged to the Oxford Mission, there was a lower or Industrial School belonging to the Society for the Propagation of the Gospel. This school, by a somewhat strange coincidence, was lodged in property belonging to the Oxford Mission. The boys, who were all Christians, came principally from the Christian families who lived in the missions of the Society for the Propagation of the Gospel in the Sunderbans—a country district south of Calcutta, of which we shall very shortly have occasion to speak. Hitherto the two schools had been taught apart, but in this year Mr. Brown built a new set of class-rooms, and arranged for both the schools, which were mostly doing the same work, to be taught together. This brought up the different classes to a much more satisfactory size, and enabled one staff of teachers to do what had formerly been the work of two.

The printing-press, which had been brought by Mr. Willis, was at this time brought into the college compound, and several of the elder boys in the Industrial School were taught the work of compositors. This Industrial School was under the charge of the Rev. M. L. Ghose, who had himself been trained at Bishop's College. He had already held the post of head master for several years, and has continued in the same responsible position ever since, fulfilling the duties of his charge with admirable sympathy, ability, and zeal.

It must be remembered that Bishop's College was, and still is, the only College in Calcutta at which students are resident, and that all the students are Christians. From it, year by year, men are sent out well educated, and with a real training in Christian Faith and life, and thus should be, in their different spheres of work, living centres of Christian influence to others. A writer in the *Epiphany*, speaking of the college in 1895, says:

" In Bishop's College, Calcutta, Christianity has welded into one representatives of almost every caste, creed, and race which is to be found in India. Here, and here only, as far as we know, are such diverse elements to be found dwelling together in harmony, and we do not know how under any other conditions than those of Christianity such union is possible. That here, too, ' union is strength,' at least in some departments of effort, is shown by the fact that during the past season the college has won the Elliott shield for football, the Lansdowne shield for cricket, and the Viceroy's medal for athletic sports—the three highest prizes open to native competition."

Here, then, in the schools and the college there existed as early as 1890 a system of education which as a framework was fairly complete. Down in the villages in the Sunderbans were a number of village schools, very primitive, perhaps, but suited to the wants of the people. From there the more intelligent boys are often sent to the Industrial School at Calcutta, and the girls to a somewhat similar school, established by the Clewer Sisters, not far from Bishop's College. Those boys, again, who show special ability pass from the Industrial School to the High School, and in due course to the college and to the University examinations. Thus the Mission can carry a boy through all the stages of his education, from the village school to the B.A. degree of the Calcutta University, keeping him the whole time in its own schools and under Christian discipline and teaching. Writing of the results of this system in 1891, when it had reached a far less efficient state than that to which it has now attained, Mr. Whitehead said:

" The whole of this branch of our work is a thoroughly satisfactory one. It is capable, no doubt, of very great improvement and extension; but even now, after seven years of more or less preparatory work in laying the foundation of a system of education for native Christians, I can see the beneficial

effects of what has already been done, in the life
of the native Church. We are gradually gathering
round us a body of young men whom we have
trained ourselves, and who are becoming themselves
most valuable fellow-helpers. Indeed, it would be
impossible to carry on our present work were it not
for their aid and co-operation."

In October of this same year another important
educational work was undertaken by the Mission
at the earnest request of the Diocesan Board of
Education—namely the charge of S. James's School
for Eurasians in Calcutta. It has fairly good buildings and a good-sized playing-field; but it is poorly
endowed, and the school fees are low and cannot
well be raised. This has crippled the school in
many ways, and among others has made it difficult
to provide a really competent staff. It was this
difficulty which led the Diocesan Board of Education to ask the Oxford Mission to undertake the
management of the school. The Mission was not
very desirous of acceding to the request; but at
the time it seemed as if the school would collapse
unless they came to the rescue. Mr. Peach therefore accepted the post of Rector, which he held till
his return to England in 1896. During his tenure
of office the numbers of the school increased considerably, and a good deal was done by way of
improvement to the playing-ground and buildings,
as well as to the general organization of the school.
Three laymen came to work with him—Mr. Conway
and Mr. Franklin in 1891, and Mr. Woodward in
1892—all of whom have since been ordained. Mr.

Woodward, to the great regret of his fellow-workers, was forbidden by the doctors to remain in India. In 1897 the Bishop of Calcutta secured a new Rector for the school, who, being a married man, was unable to join the Brotherhood; and it was thought best, in the interest of the school and the Mission alike, that the connection between the two should be severed. S. James's School was then some-what of an episode in the history of the Mission. It is the only real Church of England school of that class in Calcutta, and is therefore an important work—important not only as a means of giving a good Church education to the class of boys for whom it is meant, but also from a missionary point of view; for the Eurasians, being connected by their mixed parentage with both Europeans and natives, ought, if properly trained and imbued with real missionary zeal, to display qualities and sympathies which might form a valuable link between the two races.

A much larger work was the charge of the Sunderbans Mission, which was also taken over by the Oxford Mission in this year at the request of the Bishop. The district to which this name, meaning the "forest of the Sunder tree," is given, extends fifty miles south of Calcutta, and is about fifty miles broad. Nearly the whole of it is occupied by rice-fields, and is thickly studded with small villages at distances of about a mile apart. The country is absolutely flat and very swampy, inter-sected in all directions by innumerable small canals, which take the place of roads, and are the chief means of communication. For about five months in the year it is entirely flooded—a physical condition well suited to the cultivation of rice, which is the staple product of the district. Scattered over this area there are some three thousand Christians belonging to our own Church, and there are five or six thousand more belonging to the Roman Catholics, Baptists, and Congregationalists. Nowhere do the divisions of Christendom produce more disastrous results than among these poor and ignorant villagers; and one among the many evils which the Mission found arising from these unhappy divisions was the constant passing of the native Christians from one religious body to another.

The people are, as might be expected, very dull and slow, what energy they have being absorbed in the struggle with debt and malaria. The one thing which seems to awaken their intellectual powers is a lawsuit, which has an extraordinary attraction for them. The difficulties of the situation had been much increased by the continued ill-health of the one S.P.G. missionary who was available for the district, and who had consequently been unable to superintend the work of the catechists, and of the schools and native teachers, with the result that the machinery of the Mission had got into great disorder. When the Society for the Propagation of the Gospel withdrew this, their last available missionary, the Oxford Brotherhood felt they could not refuse the request of the Bishop to undertake the superintendence of the district. Mr. Brown was accordingly appointed to give a general

supervision to the whole, while Mr. Moore under-
took the work of itinerating among the villages,
holding services, inspecting the schools, and generally
promoting the spiritual and temporal welfare of the
people. To this work he devoted himself till April,
1894, when he was suddenly ordered home by the
doctor, on account of trouble with his eyesight,
which was largely due to the unselfish way in which
he had given himself to the exposure and hardships
incidental to the work of a missionary in such a
country. By far the larger part of his time was
spent travelling from village to village—when there
was sufficient water, by boats of various kinds and
sizes; at other times walking across the half-dried
fields which the flood had left, in the blazing heat
of the sun. The food and lodging in the district
were often of the roughest; and, as the present
writer can vouch from his own observation, the
travelling equipage which Mr. Moore considered
sufficient was of the most rudimentary kind—an
article which was broken or which no one else
thought good enough to use being appropriated
by him with enthusiasm. But if his camp-baggage
would have shocked the sense of propriety of a
third-class native servant, his work was of the
first quality; and it was his persistent self-devotion
and self-denial, his deep and earnest religiousness
and conception of duty, which were mainly the
means of raising the Missions out of the miserable
condition into which they had fallen, and which
encouraged and inspired all who worked with him.
It was a matter of deep regret that the doctors

held out no hopes of his being able to return to the work; but it gave him the opportunity for fulfilling a wish which had been for some time in his heart, namely, of offering himself to the Society of S. John the Evangelist at Cowley. Since then he has been professed and his health sufficiently restored for him to be able to work again in India, in the Fathers' admirable Mission at Poona.

One other reason which led the Oxford Mission to take up this work was the fact that Miss Hoare, who for many years had spent and been spent in the cause of the Sunderban Christians, had at last laid down her life for their sake. If the life and work in the country were rough and hard for a man, they were in every sense far more so for a lady; yet year after year Miss Hoare never shrunk back from, or wearied of, the ministry she had undertaken for the people of the district. If she had not been irresistibly drawn out to India by her love for them, in all human probability her life would have been spared. The Oxford Mission therefore felt that they could not allow a work which had been so nobly done to drop. It is also true to add that though the effort was undoubtedly a strain on the Mission staff, yet in some ways it afforded a wholesome change from the somewhat trying work among the Calcutta students, and, moreover, was a means of bringing the Mission into touch with what are in many respects the main problems of missionary work in India—namely, work in the country districts; for it must be remem-

bered that more than ninety per cent. of the population live in the country, the town population being
a mere fraction of the whole.

A good idea of the life and character of this
district is given in the following account, written by
Mr. Brown in 1891 :

"'The Sunderbans' is the name given to the
district of the Ganges delta south of Calcutta. The
whole district, and, indeed, the ground on which
Calcutta itself stands, is simply a theft from the
Himalaya mountains, the thieves being the two
great rivers Ganges and Brahmapûtra. Suppose a
fleet of thirteen thousand ships starting every
morning from the base of the mountains and each
ship discharging a daily burden of fourteen hundred
tons of earth into the Bay of Bengal, and you have
a picture of what is going on here throughout the
rainy season. And this work, it has been calculated,
must have been in progress for thirteen thousand
six hundred years to build up the present delta
three hundred feet from the bottom of the sea.
Land formed in such a way has many engaging
qualities. In the first place it is not so much land
as mud, caked over by the sun, no doubt, at certain
seasons of the year, but with a natural tendency to
revert to its original consistency whenever a fall
of rain (and the rain does fall!) gives it an excuse.
Then also it has a way of disappearing rather more
rapidly than it came. For instance, at a place
called Goalanda, in 1875, the railway station stood
near the river, protected by massive embankments,
on which £130,000 had been spent. In the August

MISSION SHALTI (CANAL BOAT).

[To face p. 46.

of that year, however, the river took a fancy to that railway station, and deep water now covers its site. Another characteristic of the country is that it is absolutely flat, and is everywhere intersected by large and small canals. The natural features of the Sunderbans therefore present rather serious obstacles to getting about. There are hardly any roads; the substitutes for them are ridges of mud banked up between the rice-fields, and these have a habit of breaking down and leaving a vast slough to wade through before you can land on the next ridge. Of course, the natives find little difficulty about it, for with their scanty clothing it does not much matter to them whether their path is through wet or dry; but the European finds himself terribly discounted by his civilization. As long as the rains last he gets on well enough in his *shalti*—something like a narrowed and elongated punt, specially adapted for these small and narrow canals—but towards the end of October he finds the canals begin to dry up. 'Capital!' thinks he; 'now I shall be able to walk.' But the fields which are too dry for punting may still be a good deal too wet for walking. If, casting away his civilization, he adopts the manners and customs of the natives, and plunges barefooted into the mud, the result is probably a sore foot, possibly a snake bite, and almost certainly a fever. If in despair he betakes himself to a horse, the rains are upon him again, and the horse has to be consigned to the stable, where it will eat its head off for the next four or five months.

" Another difficulty consists in the fact that every

single thing which you want must be taken with
you. This difficulty does not occur to people at
home, who naturally say, ' Put up at an inn.' But
there are no inns. And the condition of the country
as regards means of accommodation can be gathered
from the following description of the life of an
Indian peasant, which is evidently that of an eye-
witness :

"'A fairly contented Indian peasant or artisan
usually seems to Western eyes to possess no comforts
at all. His cottage, or rather hut, consists practically
of a single room, often (always, in our district)
built of dried mud instead of brick, with no floor,
no attempt at a chimney, the fuel used being char-
coal, and no furniture except sometimes a *charpoy*
or two—i.e., the simplest form of trestle-bed—two
or three brass *lotahs*, and some unglazed earthen
cooking-pots. There are no chairs, no carpets, no
tables for eating, no bedding in the English sense,
nothing whatever on which a British pawnbroker
would in an hour of expansiveness advance three
shillings. The owner's clothing may be worth five
shillings if he has a winter garment, and his wife's
perhaps ten shillings more, her festival robe having
a distinct value. The children wear nothing at all.
The man never sees or thinks about meat of any
kind. He never dreams of buying alcohol in any
shape. The food of the household costs about six
shillings a month, and consists of roasted rice or
unleavened cakes, fish if procurable, vegetables, milk,
and a little clarified butter, the whole being made
tasteful with cheap country spices; and his only

TWO MEN DRAWING WATER FROM A POND. SMALL BOYS CATCHING FISH WITH BASKETS

luxury is sugar, made up—sometimes cleverly, sometimes horribly, according to the *cing* of each district
—into sweetmeats.'

" Two things, and two things only, can usually be
bought in the villages—rice and kerosene oil ; two
other things you can generally borrow—a roof over
your head and a grass mat to place under you.
There are also generally one or two houses in each
village which can produce a kerosene oil-box for
a seat. For everything else you are dependent
on what you bring with you—your bed, your
bedding, your food, your cooking-vessels, your
fuel, even your water—for though there is 'water,
water everywhere,' there is not a drop that is wholesome to drink.

" In some thirty of these villages, scattered over
an area which measures about fifty miles each way,
are to be found between two and three thousand
Christians of our Church, besides Roman Catholics,
Baptists, and Methodists. A lady who has worked
in the district, triumphing over all its difficulties, for
fifteen years, describes her work as turning mud
images into human beings. And that is about what
it is. Though so near to Calcutta, their existence
is hardly recognized by the dwellers in the metropolis. A sportsman comes down now and then in
search of a tiger, and the Government has made
some small beginnings of education; but for the
most part they are both literally and metaphorically
in the mud, out of which they have neither power
nor courage to help themselves. The missionaries
have done more for them than anybody, and yet

H

after forty years of Christianity it seems as if there were still almost everything to do. To say that, however, is not quite fair. They have their own virtues, the virtues of simple and very dependent country people.

"Speaking now of our Christians: one of the first things that struck me about them was a freedom from gross vice which would compare very favourably with most country parishes in England. And along with this—though I should scarcely like to take it by itself as a sign of religious progress—is the fact that there is scarcely a man or woman in the whole district who is of age to be a communicant that is not so. Most communicate whenever they have an opportunity: all at the great festivals of the Church.

"Ignorance is our great enemy. Not more than one or two in a village know how to read and write. At the Church services there is painful silence where the responses ought to come. I have called up a lad working in the fields, ascertained that he was a Christian, and then asked whether he could say the Lord's Prayer. He did not even know what I meant. As a rule the girls know more than the boys, thanks to the noble work of Miss Hoare, whom I have already mentioned. But then the girls have a peculiar difficulty—nothing will induce them to open their lips in the presence of a man, not even in church. 'I suffer not a woman to speak,' is interpreted by them in its strictest literal significance. Our boys' schools are in a most backward state, and it will be our chief

FAMILY COOKING OUT OF DOORS IN THE COURTYARD OF A VILLAGE HOUSE
IN THE SUNDERBANS.

[To face p. 50.

work, for many years to come, to get them into a state of efficiency. Fortunately the foundation has been laid, for in the boarding-school which has now been going on for some years in Calcutta there is a large proportion of these Sunderban boys who, when they leave school, will be far more competent teachers than any we have had yet.

"Another effect of their ignorance is, that they pass almost without a thought from one Christian body to another. The Roman priest comes at a time of want and offers to lend them money, and immediately they become Roman Catholics. They have a quarrel with the reader, and they pass over to the Baptists. So little individuality have they that if one member of the family goes to another body, all the members of the family, whether children or adults, go with him. The fact is, that the traditions of Hindu caste still cling to them. The whole effect of caste is to destroy individuality, to take away the capacity of thinking for oneself, to substitute a body of external rules for the inner voice of conscience, to make all the members of the caste move like the serried ranks of an army without the possibility of any one asserting an opinion of his own. What wonder if the age-long influence of this system is still felt after a generation or two of Christianity! The Christians themselves tend to become a separate caste, with rules a little different, no doubt, from those of the Hindus, but enforced by the same sanctions of fine and excommunication; and when once this deadly spirit creeps in, the work of the conversion of the heathen is entirely forgotten, and it gets to be looked upon almost as a thing impossible that a Hindu should forsake his own caste and enter the Christian Church. This is the most striking defect in the Christianity of these people : they scarcely even dream of making converts; the missionary spirit is entirely dead.

"Education, then, and the rekindling of a missionary spirit is what we chiefly want. My great hope is that we shall be able to reorganize our village schools, to establish boarding-schools for boys and girls in their midst, to train the native readers and pastors until they become leaders in the cause of aggressive Christianity. All this is the work of time, not of just one or two years. One can scarcely hope to see it accomplished in one's own lifetime; but we can now be working towards it and making it easier for our successors to bring it about. 'Show Thy servants Thy work, and their children Thy glory,' must be our motto as well as our prayer.

"Our work amongst the Christians is very like parish work at home—visiting the people, getting them to send their children to school, inspecting the schools, and holding services. But in every village there is sure to be a greater or less proportion of Hindus and Mussulmans. For them a magic-lantern has been immensely useful. When due notice has been given, the people flock to see it, and in this way we have had audiences of some three thousand in all, in about fifteen different places, during the cold weather. We always show the life of CHRIST,

Bamboo Bridge over a Canal in the Sunderbans.

and I generally take with me a student of Bishop's
College, named Okhil Sinjh, formerly in our school,
who preaches most excellently on the various scenes,
and accompanies his preaching with the singing of
Bengali hymns to the tune of his violin, which is
intensely appreciated. In this way I hope that
much good is being done, though we have not as
yet seen any definite fruit in the way of conversion.
I cannot speak too highly of the qualities of the
lantern : it packs into a very small space, and yet
gives a disc of some eight feet, which is quite large
enough for all our purposes. The people quickly
rig up a framework of bamboos in the open air, on
which we hang our sheet. At one place we set it
up in this way between the church and a road—one
of the few roads of the district ; and when all the
people of the village had settled themselves on one
side, under the shadow of the church, the pictures
could also be seen on the other side by people
passing along the road. It happened to be a market day, and the people going home from market
invariably stopped to look, so that in this way
we got an attendance of some four hundred.

"On another occasion a Hindu station-master
asked us to give an exhibition at his station, and
promised us a large attendance, 'six hundred, at
least,' he said. We fixed the day, and went at the
time appointed, and there we found indeed the
station-master himself and his family, but 'not the
six hundred.' His excuse was characteristic : 'Oh,
I never thought you would come when you said you
would.' However, by ringing the railway bell and

sending messengers right and left, he managed to muster a respectable audience in about an hour, and we had a very successful exhibition. When it was all over and it was nearly midnight, a few laggards arrived, and suggested that we should begin it again! We could only promise to return at some future time."

In both the pastoral and evangelistic work in this district Mr. Brown and Mr. Moore were helped by the Rev. B. C. Chowdry, an old S.P.G. missionary who gave his services voluntarily, and by the Rev. M. L. Ghose and other Bengali fellow-workers. And, under the firm and wise discipline exercised by the Oxford Mission, every year saw steady and real improvement, and in 1893, out of 3,345 baptized persons, 1,442 were communicants. These were distributed in ninety-three villages, for the use of which were three churches, twenty-nine chapels, and twenty-five schools, which were served, in addition to the two members of the Oxford Mission and three or four Bengali priests, by eleven readers and twenty-five schoolmasters. It is a work which needs patient and continuous toil, but one which will repay the labour bestowed upon it.

CHAPTER IV

THE NEW MISSION HOUSE

" Not throned above the skies,
    Not golden-wall'd afar,
But where CHRIST's two or three
    In His Name gathered are.
Be in the midst of them
    GOD's own Jerusalem! "

IT will have been seen that the year 1890 was a
year in which the sphere of the Mission was
considerably extended, and that it was now in a
position to offer a great variety of work to any one
who would join it. At the Mission House there
was the regular work among the students, consisting
principally of individual intercourse and visiting
them in their clubs and lodgings. Here, too, in
the cold weather was an opportunity for giving
lectures to non-Christians, while the *Epiphany*
afforded scope for a considerable amount of literary
ability. The schools and Bishop's College offered
different grades of educational work, from the
teaching of elementary subjects up to lectures for
the University examinations; while in the oversight
of the native congregations in Calcutta and the
Missions in the Sunderbans was to be found
abundance of ordinary pastoral work, besides that
of a direct missionary kind.

From time to time, as opportunity occurred, lectures were given at Patna and at Dacca, and requests also came for lectures from as far away as Poona and Bombay. Their annual holiday afforded the members of the Mission the opportunity of visiting other parts of India and gaining fresh experience by seeing missionary efforts of different kinds. Thus in 1889 Mr. Walker visited Burmah, and in 1890 Mr. Peach made a very interesting tour among the flourishing Christian villages in South India. We mention this because it is important that it should be understood that by means of the variety of the work there is ample room in the Mission for men of very different gifts and capacities, and also that the wide extent of its responsibilities and opportunities does very urgently call for a much larger staff of men.

It is the constant fluctuation in the numbers of the Mission which is one of the great anxieties connected with the work, and which imperatively calls for a considerable increase in the permanent number of men. There is, we believe, an impression, still strong, that only men of great intellectual ability are wanted. This is an entire mistake. While the highest intellectual gifts will find ample scope for their exercise, they are not by any means the chief or only gifts required. Such qualities as go to make an ordinary good parish priest at home, backed by a real vocation to missionary work, are what are really needed. No one who has these qualifications need be afraid of not finding plenty of work, and work of as much interest as any at home.

OXFORD MISSION HOUSE, CORNWALLIS STREET, CALCUTTA.

[*To face p.* 57.

The most important event of this year was undoubtedly the opening of the new Mission House in Cornwallis Street. This eventually took place on Wednesday, November 25, 1891, with a special service of blessing by the Bishop and in the presence of a large company of lay and clerical friends.

The house, which is a large, oblong building, stands with its west end facing upon Cornwallis Street—a large street, which under various names runs right through the centre of Calcutta. Its situation is an ideal one for the special work of the Mission. It is almost exactly in the centre of the students' lodgings, and hundreds of students pass and repass it every day on their way to and from the colleges. The advantage of this more public position was seen in the largely increased attendance of students at the lectures. In the new house it was found practicable to maintain a course of weekly lectures for ten weeks during the cold weather, with a regular audience of from one hundred and fifty to two hundred men.

Being planned especially for the Mission, the house is, in all its arrangements, admirably adapted for its purpose; and the excellence of its construction was shown in the fact that in the somewhat severe shock of earthquake which caused so much damage in Calcutta in 1897, the Mission House received no injury whatever. It is, as will be seen from the illustration, a large three-storied building, plain but dignified, built, as are all Calcutta buildings, of brick and stucco. The floors throughout the house are made of a kind of very smooth cement, which can be easily washed over with water, and which helps very much in the way of cleanliness and coolness—in fact, it is quite one of the coolest houses in Calcutta. The main entrance is under a porch at the west end of the house, facing Cornwallis Street, which leads into a large hall open to the top of the house, from which a broad staircase leads up to the different stories, from the ground-floor to the roof. On the ground-floor, besides two or three rooms, one of which is sometimes used as a students' club-room, there is the "Liddon Lecture Hall." This was so called because it was built with a legacy of £250 which was left by Dr. Liddon to the Mission at his death. Dr. Liddon had from the very first taken the warmest interest in the Mission, and had done much to help it on during its earlier stages by his sympathy and advice. It was felt, therefore, to be singularly appropriate that the room which was to be devoted to lectures, the aim of which was to bring home to the hearts of the young educated Bengalis the claim of JESUS CHRIST, should bear the name of one who for twenty years had, with unrivalled eloquence and deepest devotion, proclaimed that Name from the pulpit of S. Paul's Cathedral in the City of London. The lecture-room is capable of holding nearly three hundred people, and with the club-room, which can be added to it, and the wide corridor into which it opens, could accommodate some five hundred to hear a lecture. At the east end is a small apse, which is screened off from the main room, but which can be fitted with an altar, and thus enable the room to be used

Liddon Lecture Room fitted as Chapel for the Festival.

[*To face p.* 58.

as a chapel on such occasions as the annual festival, when the number of visitors is too great for the ordinary chapel upstairs.

On the first floor there are three rooms for the use of the Brethren, and at the other end a very fine room, as large as the lecture-hall below, which serves as library, common-room, and refectory in one. It is absolutely plain, but lofty and well proportioned, which, with its size, gives it a real dignity. The walls are entirely lined with book-cases, which contain the Mission House library; and some idea of the difference between the present house and that in Muktaram Babu Street may be gained from the fact that the bookcases, which in the old house used to touch the ceiling, now only reach half-way up the walls.

It need not be pointed out how valuable a good library is to such a body as the Brotherhood of the Epiphany, the members of which have to be dealing continually with every kind of intellectual problem, and to whom not only inquirers but clergy and others are constantly referring on social and theo-logical questions. It is, then, very important that the library should be kept efficient by a continual supply of new books, and for this purpose a list of books which are wanted is published in each quarterly paper, which can be obtained of any of the local secretaries of the Mission.

Between the library and the other rooms on this floor is the chapel, the centre of the house as well as of the life and work of the Brotherhood. It is in a way unique of its kind, being, we believe, the

first specimen of Mr. Kempe's work which was seen
in India. All the woodwork, which is of teak, was
made in England under Mr. Kempe's own supervision, and sent out to Calcutta, where it was fitted
and placed in the chapel. It consists of panelling
for the entire walls up to the height of nine or ten
feet, of plain but handsome stalls, and a very
beautifully designed reredos, the pattern of which is
brought out with great effect by a few touches of
gilding. The whole gives a combination of good
taste and quiet solemnity, carrying one back in
thought to some chapel of an Oxford college, and
is a perpetual rest and spiritual refreshment. All
the woodwork was the generous gift of the late Mr.
Wakeman, then treasurer of the Mission, and forms
only one of his many benefactions to the Brotherhood. Many other beautiful gifts, such as vestments,
altar-frontals, silver sanctuary lamps, have been
given from time to time by members of the
Association. The chalice and paten were the gift
of Mrs. King, the mother of the Bishop of Lincoln.[1]
Thus the chapel is full of memories of those who
have thought and prayed for the work; but one
memory pervades it above all, that of Marsham
Frederick Argles, of whom the chapel itself is a
memorial—a memorial which is indeed fitting for
one in the life of whom prayer and worship formed
so great and real a part. Here the Brethren meet

[1] The chalice was stolen in the early part of this year,
1899—a great loss, both on account of the beauty of the
vessel itself and of the associations which attached to it
from the donor.

OXFORD MISSION CHAPEL, CALCUTTA.

[To face p. 60.

throughout the day to recite the Divine Office and to say "the Hours"; and here, above all, is offered each day the Holy Eucharist—the daily thanksgiving for all GOD has given to, and done through, the Mission; and the daily pleading of the one all-sufficient and all-prevailing Sacrifice, for the conversion of India. In the larger and truer view which belongs to the unseen world may it not be that this is recognized as the most real and fruitful of all the work which the Mission is doing? Anyhow, in those times which must come again and again in all missionary efforts, when the sense of failure and disappointment lie heavy on the soul, and the long toil seems to bring no result, hope rekindles and recovers strength as morning by morning the great Sacrifice is pleaded, the memorial of Him Who said, "I, if I be lifted up, will draw all men unto Me"; carrying with it the promise that the prayer shall indeed be answered, and that the hearts of the children in India shall at last be turned to the FATHER of all.

The top story is entirely occupied with rooms for the members of the Brotherhood. All the rooms on each floor open on to a wide and lofty verandah, which from its great length and width is quite imposing. Facing south, the house gets the full benefit of the south wind, which in the hot weather blows most refreshingly all night. From the top story a staircase leads up to the roof, which, like that of all Eastern houses, is flat, and is in constant use for a variety of purposes. This roof is, we believe, large enough for a full-sized tennis-court—

it was, we know, at times used as a skating-rink
for roller-skates! Standing high above all the
surrounding buildings, it commands an extensive
view of almost the whole of Calcutta, and after a
hot day's work it is a refreshing place for sitting or
walking when the sun has set. Very wonderful it
is at night to stand there and to look up into the
clear sky, in which the great stars shine with a
brilliancy unknown in our heavier and damper
climate ; and then to look over the great heathen
city, so unconscious of, nay, as yet so indifferent
to, the real meaning of the heavens which night
after night declare to it the glory of GOD—that
city, in the middle of which the Mission House
stands like some point of vantage, from which is
to go forth the message which is to win it to
the Faith of CHRIST.

Year by year at the feast of the Epiphany an
increasing number of English and Indian Christian
friends meet at the Mission House to keep with
the Brethren their annual festival. Here, too,
throughout the year welcome visitors come from
time to time—missionaries passing through Calcutta,
apprentices from the ships lying in the port, soldiers
from Fort William, members of the Civil Service,
officers in the Army, travellers who are spending
the cold weather in India. Many an English layman
who has taken the trouble to come down the somewhat rough and unsavoury streets from the European
end of Calcutta to pay the Mission a visit has very
likely never thought of the encouragement and help
which his bright, cheery presence has been.

Not only did the move into the new house show results in a largely increased and more regular attendance at the weekly lectures, but it seemed to bring to the Mission a different class of inquirers from those with whom it had come in contact in previous years. They were both intellectually more able and also more in earnest, and the Superior reported that they had more catechumens this year than the Mission had had during the whole ten years of its previous history. There did seem just at this time a very apparent movement towards Christianity: though at the time Mr. Whitehead expressly said that it would be rash to assert that it was more than a passing wave of feeling. To gauge the depth or reality of such movements is always very difficult, and later events came to show that, however real it was at the time, it was not lasting; and in a few years it became evident that a strong reaction antagonistic to Christianity was taking place. This arose partly from a political feeling opposed to anything English, and partly from an attempted revival of orthodox Hinduism. But of this we shall have to speak later on.

The large increase of work which had come to the Mission during the last three years had put a heavy burden on its resources, and in the earlier months of this year the strain upon the staff was very great. The numbers of the Mission, though larger than they had been before, were not large enough for the work, which was on all sides opening out; and at the end of 1891 and beginning of 1892 they were further reduced through the necessary absence of Mr. Walker and Mr. Peach; and for the moment it did seem as if it might be necessary for the Mission to retrace its steps. This is obviously a condition in which no Mission ought ever to be. If a work is a living work and is blest of GOD, it must grow, and therefore must need a continual increase both of funds and of men. The responsibility for the supply of these needs lies with the Church at home. We could wish that the Church realized her responsibility more fully. Apart from many other considerations, this ought to be prominently brought before Churchmen: that the mortality in Missions, especially in such a Mission as that of the Universities' Mission to Central Africa, is very largely due to over-pressure—to the fact that every man is overworked, and that, in that state, illnesses which might otherwise have been easily thrown off are constantly fatal. It is really the negligence and apathy of the Church at home which is the cause of so many deaths in the mission-field. Thanks to Miss Murray and the generosity of the Association in England, the financial needs of the Mission were always met. But for a time the weakness of the staff caused very real anxiety. However, relief came in time. Mr. Walker returned in July, and Mr. Peach, who had been delayed in England through an attack of illness, came out in November; and what was more, three new members arrived the same month—the Rev. Edward Manley, S. John's College, Cambridge; the Rev. Frederick Wingfield Douglass, Christ Church, Oxford, and Curate of S. Pancras; and

the Rev. George Longridge. Mr. Manley and
Mr. Longridge were with the Mission for only
two years, but Mr. Douglass has been a permanent
addition to the staff.

CHAPTER V

THE CALCUTTA UNIVERSITY

" For the worst of us to say they have so seen;
For the better what it was they saw; the best
Impart the gift of seeing to the rest."

" THE present phase of education in India,"
writes Bishop Gore, " may be said to date
from Lord Macaulay's famous minute in 1835.
Before his arrival in India the Committee of Public
Instruction had been divided, five against five, on
the question whether the Government should continue to subsidize, regulate, and extend the old
Oriental learning, in Sanscrit, Persian, and Arabic,
as they had been doing hitherto, or whether all this
should be swept away in favour of English education.

" ' The advocates of the two systems,' Sir George
Trevelyan tells us in his *Life of Lord Macaulay*,
' laid their opinions before the supreme council;
and Macaulay, as a member of that council, produced a minute in favour of the latter view which
set the question at rest at once and for ever.' It
said all that he was so well qualified to say on
the greatness of English literature and science, and
heaped ridicule on the literature and science of
India—on its ' medical doctrines, which would dis-

grace an English farrier; astronomy, which would move laughter in the girls at an English boarding-school; history, abounding with kings thirty feet high, and reigns thirty thousand years long; and geography made up of seas of treacle and seas of butter.' He pointed out with great richness of illustration how in modern Europe at the Renaissance and in Russia, within the last hundred and twenty years, we had had numerous instances of a great impulse given to the mind of a whole society, of prejudice overthrown, of knowledge diffused, of taste purified, of arts and sciences planted in countries which had recently been ignorant and barbarous, by the propagation of a foreign literature in place of the old national one. 'The language of Western Europe civilized Russia; I cannot doubt that they will do for the Hindu what they have done for the Tartar.'

"So it was decided. A thoughtful man might well have had his doubts whether all the contempt that Macaulay poured in this and other writings of his on Oriental literature and religion was not a good deal too much the contempt of utter unsympathy, the unsympathy of a utilitarian disposition with the whole temper of the East. Since his days there has been a reaction. But in any case such was the decision, and Macaulay's biographer records the splendid success, as measured by statistics, which has attended the movement then inaugurated.

"What have been its results in the past fifty years? We may, perhaps, summarize them in this way:

" First, there has been an immense superficial diffusion among the large classes who come under the influence of the University education of the ideas and terms of modern Europe.   If you talk to the students at the University in Calcutta, or if you are called upon to preside over some of the debates held in their clubs, you hear all the phrases with which you are familiar in ' liberal ' England. The ideas might have come straight from leading articles in newspapers, or from Macaulay's *Essays*, or from the tracts of Mr. Bradlaugh, Mrs. Besant, or Colonel Ingersoll.   The names of Mill and Herbert Spencer and Bain, of Lecky and Buckle, of Coleridge and Carlyle are ' household words.'

" Secondly, this superficial acquaintance with modern European ideas has had a destructive, but very little intellectual or spiritual reconstructive effect.   The old idolatrous superstitions cannot live in their atmosphere.   They wither and lose force. It is equally destructive to the old brooding, speculative, subtle, metaphysical, and pantheistic philosophy of the Hindu.   And if its ' enlightenment ' and its utilitarian modes of thought have undermined the forces of superstitious worship and meditative philosophy, scarcely less has its individualism acted as a powerful solvent upon the strong ties and restraints of the old social ' caste ' system of India.   The familiarity with modern ideas, then, has had a destructive effect upon Hindu worship and metaphysics and social obligations, but very little reconstructive effect.   The students are mostly sceptical, without being much more.   The Theistic movement,

of which a good deal was heard at home in connection with the visit to England of Keshub
Chunder Sen, one of its founders, which is eclectic
—that is, which is an attempt 'to take the best
out of all religious systems,' and which uses a good
deal of Christian language, and professes a great
deal of Christian belief—excites among the more
earnest students a great deal of interest, but not
apparently any of the enthusiasm of self-committal
which would lead them to enrol themselves as
actual members of the 'Somaj' or association. So
strongly has the Government felt recently the
disastrous effect on morals of the merely secular
education, that an educational committee has
recently endeavoured to procure the establishment
of a text-book of moral principles such as all good
men would agree upon. But what is wanted is not
principles—in the sense of ideas and maxims—but
motives which should stimulate and appeal to the
will and conscience, such motives as cannot come
out of a text-book.

"Thirdly, the effect of European education has
been apparently to produce a great gulf between
the outer idea and language and the inner self of
the Hindu student. His outer language and stock-
in-trade is mostly modern, more or less blatant,
utilitarian scepticism or eclectic Theism. But underneath—far underneath the English-speaking exterior
—sometimes, perhaps, almost unknown to himself,
there lives and works, silent and uncommunicative,
the old Hindu self, impenetrable, reserved, inacces-
sible, unsatisfied in a world where it cannot find

its home, where GOD does not mean it to find
its home."

It is in this sort of world that some six thousand
students live in Calcutta. Outside the lecture-room
the staff of the University exercises no control whatever over them. There is no proctorial system,
no licensing of lodgings, no supervision of any
kind. It is true that many of the students live
in their own homes in Calcutta, but a large number
are young men whose homes are away in the
country, and who are consequently thrown among
all the temptations of a great city, absolutely uncared for, at an age when sympathy, with guidance
and proper discipline, are what they most need.
The wonder is that the tone of the students is as
good as it is. But the system is a miserable one
and thoroughly bad in its effects.

How, then, do the students live who have not
their home in Calcutta, or who do not board with
friends or relations? They live in what are called
"messes"—that is, in houses holding sometimes as
many as forty students, sometimes as few as ten
or a dozen. As a rule the smaller messes are
the best. The houses which are utilized for this
purpose are in the close neighbourhood of the
colleges, and are to be found in College and
Cornwallis Streets, and in the lanes running at all
angles out of those thoroughfares.

"A mess is formed on various principles —
sometimes on the basis of common friendship,
sometimes on that of being at the same college,
or in the same year of their University course, or

because they belong to the same village or district. But beyond this there is one thing which regulates all else in the formation of a mess, and that is financial capacity. The student as a rule is of very limited means, and he cannot afford to live except with those whose income is on the same scale as his own. Caste does not so much enter into the matter: for the cook can always be a Brahman, and, therefore, not only prepares food fit for a Brahman student, but also for every one else; and if the Brahman student commences to eat his food in the common dining-room the infinitesimal fraction of a minute before the non-Brahman students, the exigencies of caste are preserved. A body of students, having agreed to mess together, next proceed to secure a house. A six or seven-roomed two-storied house is the average size, though some are much bigger. Seven rooms represent accommodation for many more than seven students, as two or three students generally share a room. A house such as this would be secured for between forty or fifty rupees a month. On the lower floor the cooking is done, and there, too, the dining-room is situated. A table, with benches running round it, is the regulation type in the more civilized abodes; in others the inmates sit on the floor, and eat out of dishes or from leaves also placed on the floor. Up a winding, ruinous stair they go to their common room and bedrooms. The common room is the most distinctive part of the mess. Here they study, converse, receive visitors, and smoke. A stray

chair or two, a table used only when writing has
to be done, a shelf running across one side of
the room, or an aristocratic bookcase, when funds
permit, to hold their books, complete the furniture
of the room.   A rope hung across an angle of
the room acts as clothes-horse for their superfluous
garments; for in the common room they wear only
the minimum of clothing.   Here the weightiest
problems are discussed.   Students of the same
college refresh their memory as to what was said
at the college lectures; students of different colleges
compare professors' notes.   Evidence is recorded
and never forgotten; it may be erroneously con-
veyed, but it sticks.   Peculiarities are mimicked
to perfection; curious gestures, uncommon expres-
sions, occasional objurgations, a peculiar accent—
all are recorded by these critics, and coined into
history.   It is not only European professors that
are weighed in the balance and found wanting;
Bengali professors have also their peculiarities,
which are duly chronicled.   The sleeping-rooms
have even less furniture : a mat, or at best a
charpoy, with a rug or shawl or coarse blanket as
a covering in winter, are all they need.

"In students' English there is an expression,
'fooding-expenses,' which nothing will induce them
to part with.   This forms a very important item
of the expenditure of the mess.   The chief point
of agreement between all messes is quantity of
food ; quality differs in different cases.   The cook
who caters for the mess makes ends meet at the
sacrifice of the students' health ; but that is hardly

his concern. His chief concern is *dustooree*; and that he may obtain this perquisite from students who pay him five rupees a month for two full meals a day it is necessary that he shall give them the coarsest rice, rancid vegetables, and vile curry. The monthly sum, which varies from five to fifteen rupees, accounts for two meals a day—one about 9.30 or 10 a.m., and the other at 8.30 or 9 p.m. These consist of variations of rice, vegetables, curry, and fish, as the case may be. But besides these two meals, students provide themselves with tiffin independently.

" The absolutely necessary clothing of a student who is poor consists of a shirt, made in the English pattern, which is almost *de rigueur*, a *dhutee*, a *chudder*, and a pair of shoes, with the addition in the cold weather of a shawl and a pair of stockings. The shirt costs from one rupee eight annas to two rupees, according to quality. Three shirts are necessary, more are desirable. The *dhutees* may be had for about twelve annas, and the *chudder* for about the same rate. Shoes run from two rupees eight annas to five rupees, or, if the student prefers country slippers, only twelve annas. The stockings, often of an alarming mixture of colour—yellow, purple, and scarlet being a favourite combination—cost about one rupee a pair. The shawl, if of Birmingham manufacture, varies from three to five rupees; if true Indian, it costs from fifteen to fifty rupees, or even more, but this only the ' mashers' wear. This genus is not unknown among the Calcutta students. He

L

is redolent of vile perfumes, his fingers scintillate with real or sham jewels, his massive body is enswathed in costly raiment, and his empty face expresses contempt for honest poverty and simple gear.

" The house-servants are two in number. The cook attends to the bazaar, the cooking, and purveying. He gets ten rupees a month as wages. The other chief servant is a woman, who does all the housework. She has her hands full, as, in addition to washing and cleaning the house, she has to get light refreshments for the members of the mess and do odd jobs for them. She gets six or seven rupees a month. Besides these two house-servants, there is the everlasting *dhobee*, who, probably, has a hard time of it with men of limited wardrobes, as he has to make many journeys to and fro.

" Text-books mentioned in the University calendar, and note-books for taking down lectures, and 'keys' form an Indian student's library. If he is poor, he cannot afford any more. If he is rich, he does not care for any more, excepting in rare cases." [1]

This may give our readers some idea of the outward aspect of the Calcutta University, and of the material conditions under which the students live. But the influence of their material surroundings is only one among the many influences which go to form their character, and by no means

[1] Taken from an article contributed to the O.M.C. *Quarterly Paper*, July, 1894.

most powerful. Behind and beneath these mere outward things, as Bishop Gore has pointed out, lies the disintegrating force of the education which is being given to them. Few, perhaps, except those who have carefully watched what has been going on underneath the surface of education in India, have any conception of the tremendous and far-reaching moral and religious issues which are at stake, or of the change which Western education is producing in that class of the Indian people which it touches. We cannot, we think, put it more plainly than in the following extracts. The first is from a speech made by Sir Arthur Wilson at the annual meeting of the Mission in 1892. Sir Arthur held a very high position in the Indian Civil Service, and speaks out of the large experience which that position gave him. This is what he says of the result of the present system of education on the young men of India:

"It teaches the young men Western science with its accuracy, its criticism, its definitions, its careful distinguishing between the province of one subject and the province of another. It teaches them not only Western science, but it teaches them Western philosophy. It teaches them to read history through the medium of Western books. It accustoms them to read books—story-books, books of selections, and everything of that kind in which, in every page, there are ideals of conduct, implied, if not expressed, utterly different from anything that Hinduism has ever heard of before. It teaches young men the

habit of classifying and dividing, of carefully sepa-
rating that which really properly belongs to religion
and morals from that which belongs to history or
philosophy, or to questions of social organization or
social science; and by so doing it splits up, to the
mind of any one who understands the principle, the
whole of this great complicated Hindu system into
separate parts, and thereby it destroys the whole.
Then, again, English education immediately brings
to the minds which come under its influence the
habit of secularizing everything. The young Hindu
has been accustomed to regard the philosophy in
which he has been trained, and the history which
he has been taught, the social and the family systems
in which he has been brought up, as absolutely sacred
and divine, far too sacred for discussion or consideration. But the moment that he gets into his first year
in English education he finds every one of these
subjects treated as purely secular matters, to be
discussed without fear or reverence or hesitation
of any kind. In the next place, he is brought face
to face with the historical criticism of the West;
and the young man, if he has any thought at all,
will and does apply that criticism to the mythology
and to the history which he has been taught in his
childhood; and so the whole is again shaken. But,
further, not only is he taught this secular philosophy
and this critical method, but he is promptly taught
political economy as it is understood in the West,
and the various branches of social and economical
science.

"Now, reflect for a moment what all Western

economy is based on. It is based on one idea—
a strict, hard, unflinching individualism. And just
think of what the effect of that is upon the mind
of a young man who has been brought up in a joint
family, where the family labour for the joint benefit
and the property is joint property. He has been
accustomed to say of their possessions, 'This is ours.
It is the property of our family.' Teach that young
man the habit of saying, not, 'This is *ours*,' but, 'This
is *mine*,' and you have worked a revolution. I have
not time to dwell upon this further. I might point
out to you many more ways in which English
education destroys what it finds there. The effect
of all this inevitably is, that in proportion as these
young men have been trained in English-speaking
schools and colleges, in that very proportion their
old faith and their old creed grow weak; in that
very proportion their old worship and their old
ritual tend to lose their spiritual meaning; in that
very proportion all the old morality, based upon
their old creeds, loses its binding force; and all
those powerful ties based on social organization and
family system which are so tremendously powerful
in maintaining them within the limits of the recognized morality begin to lose their efficacy.

"That is surely an exceedingly serious state of
things. But the question comes next, What is being
given them by this English education in exchange
for all this morality and spiritual force, and for all
influence which it takes away? There is only one
answer, it gives nothing. It is absolutely true that,
so far as the spiritual and moral side of the young

man's character is concerned, English education is absolutely and solely negative and destructive. It gives nothing in return, there is no doubt about it. Although we may be training up from year to year batches of young men, intellectually better furnished than their fathers were; and though we may be turning them out better fitted, in some respects, to fight in the struggle for physical existence, we are turning them out morally poorer than they ever were before. To my mind I must say that this is an appalling state of things. To my mind it seems, perhaps, the most depressing and discouraging circumstance of any that now exist in connection with the administration of India; and I must say that to my knowledge there are many of the best friends of the people of India, and many of the best friends of the spread of knowledge, who would say without hesitation that it would have been far better for the people of the country if English education had never come there at all, than that it should have come, and such a price should be paid for it as the moral declension which it has brought with it. This is no new complaint that I am making. I have not said a single thing that has not been said over and over again. Every native gentleman in Calcutta, the father of a family, knows it, and laments it, and will speak freely to you about it. The newspapers (native as well as English) have written columns and columns upon it. Police officers and magistrates and judges cannot help noticing it. The departments who have to do with education have written upon it. The Government of India has recognized the evil fully. It has published, at least, one resolution on the subject, eminently virtuous and perfectly infructuous."

The second extract which we will quote is from an article written in 1896 by a Bengali gentleman, Mr. Bishan Narayan Dar. He has been speaking of the results of the present system of education on the religious and social life of his fellow-countrymen, and he concludes his article with the following words :

" Hence it is that we have a generation of young men who have no landmark on earth and no lode-star in heaven ; who have no religious convictions, no fixed moral principles, no well-defined ideals of conduct. There is no wonder, then, if Indian parents, to whom the one-sided education of their children has brought so much disappointment, turn round in bitterness and indignation to the Government and complain, as they are complaining now, 'You have taught our children science and philo-sophy; you have unrolled before their eyes the ample page of history, rich with the spoils of time—not only such as are recorded in the annals of mankind, but such as are written in letters of flame above and in the strata of the earth beneath. You call this civilization, and are proud of having communi-cated its impact to India ; but are you aware what mischief you are unwittingly doing us ? Your scientific education has made our children irreligious, atheistic, agnostic; they are beginning to look upon religion as (what one of your clever writers called it the other day) "a dream of hysterical women

and half-starved men"; they no longer believe in
the divine source of virtue, but think that it is a
proper balancing of profit and loss; they have
become irreverent, disobedient, disloyal; they have
lost all fixity of character; they are too ready to
act on the first prompting of passion and interest,
and call it independence; they boast that they
have adopted the Epicurean precept, "Eat, drink,
and be merry, for to-morrow we die and become
carbonic acid, water, and ammonia"; and they
laugh at us old men for what they mockingly call
our antediluvian notions. Surely the Iron Age has
come, for it has been said that when it comes
knowledge will be more and more, but wisdom will
be less and less. And that you Englishmen should
be the leaders of such an age is quite in accordance
with the fitness of things. You say you have given
us light, but your light is worse than darkness. We
do not thank you for it. Better far that our
children should remain ignorant of your sciences,
but retain the simple faith of their ancestors, than
that they should know all the *ologies* of the day, but
turn their back upon religion and morality as mere
rags and remnants of a superstitious age.'

"Whether we agree or not with this complaint,
which sounds ever and anon through the pæans
of joy sung over the diffusion of European civilization in India, like a passing bell across a marriage
feast, it cannot fail to arouse in us a deep, tragic
interest in the death of the old régime that must
cause disquietude, discomfort, and unhappiness to
millions on millions of men. There is no more

tragic event under the sun than the death of a
nation, and this consists in the destruction of the
beliefs, institutions, and national peculiarities that
give it an individual character. This awful tragedy
is now going on in India. The old religion is dying;
the old morality is dying; the bonds of custom
and tradition which are the bones and sinews of
the social organism are dissolving; there is death
and decomposition all around. For all this the
secular spirit of the educational system is responsible. The crisis is serious; the destiny of a nation
is at stake. A mere let-aloneist attitude will not do;
something must be done to replace that which is
passing away. If an attempt is made to face the
crisis with boldness, with promptitude, and in right
earnest, well and good; if not, matters will soon
become still more hopeless, the reins will have
been thrown upon the necks of the horses, and the
last hope of reform without revolution will be gone."

These are grave and serious words, which surely
every Englishman who cares for the welfare of India
ought to lay to heart, for they reveal a religious and
social condition among the young educated classes
which is not only deplorable in the present, but
which has in it the elements of very serious danger
for the future.

And here it is natural to ask, Why does not the
Government of India take some steps to remedy
so serious an evil? The real remedy lies, of course,
in Christianity; and there all who know India
best and who have the cause of Missions most at
heart are agreed that the Government as a govern-

M

ment must be neutral; and for this, among other
reasons, that an official recognition of Christianity
would, in the present state of India, produce a
vast number of utterly unreal conversions—of men
confessing Christianity without any conviction of its
truth or any desire to live the Christian life.

We have dwelt at length on this subject because
we feel that the real condition of things in Calcutta
is so little realized in England, and because it is just
this situation that such institutions as the Oxford
Mission can most effectively deal with. Slowly and
quietly the Brotherhood of the Epiphany have been
studying the question; year by year they have been
gaining experience, getting to see below the surface,
and to grasp the terrible condition to which the
present system has brought the mass of the students.
This experience they embodied in the following
article, which appeared in the *Epiphany* in 1895,
and which forms a most heavy and serious indict-
ment of the present condition of university education
in Calcutta :—

"Our educational system has invented a sufficiently
unnatural state of things as it is by congregating in
this metropolis and its environment a vast swarm of
youths and boys of all ages, of rudimentary morals,
and less than rudimentary religion, under no system
of supervision or discipline of any sort or kind.
That vice of every shade, nameless and shameless,
should abound is of course only what is to be
expected under the circumstances; and the results
are constantly being brought before us, sometimes
in lamentable instances of wrecked lives, shattered

physique, and damaged minds, though most of all, perhaps, in the strange and utter opaqueness in all spiritual concerns which so conspicuously characterizes the student population, and speaks all too clearly of the premature darkening that comes by an early surrender to evil.

"Meanwhile an infatuated Government goes blundering on, providing lecture-rooms and lectures and examinations in the pathetic hope of developing the talent of the country and rearing a morally competent official class. Lately it has been even so benevolent as to supply a large building for a boarding establishment in Calcutta; and though it naturally declines to equip it with the European supervision and organization requisite for maintaining something like discipline in a barrack of one hundred students, it has condescended to erect a third story, so as to lodge an additional hundred or so to swell the existing disorder, concerning which perhaps the less said the better. So we go drifting on from bad to worse, the ever-increasing numbers keeping pace with the growing degeneracy. It is a million pities that the educational future of a great country should be in the hands of the party of shallow intellectualism whose only nostrum for all the evils of mankind is bookish 'culture,' and who seem scarcely in earnest even over that. When will this pernicious superstition be outgrown? Not, we fear, till some appalling revelation opens our eyes to our insanity.

"Those who know what evils are sometimes apt to develop in public schools, even in England, under

more or less of Christian supervision, may guess
approximately what would be the result if the
youths now boarded at Eton, Harrow, and Rugby,
as well as at the Universities, were sent for their
education to London, to live promiscuously in lodgings as they pleased, with no obligations imposed
upon them beyond a certain percentage of attend-
ances at lectures ; the education, besides, being
regarded merely in the light of a step towards
employment, like that given at certain well-known
'cramming' establishments. Picture the said
students, moreover, as armed morally with little
beyond a vague consciousness of a certain impro-
priety or inexpediency in vice, with no definite
principles on the subject, and brought up, if with
any religion beyond a belief in the caste-system,
in one which canonizes impurity in its gods and
their votaries, and has no disgrace or penalties for
any but ceremonial transgressions ! Imagine them,
further, with hardly any sort of healthy amusement,
physical or mental, to ease the strain of the
crammer's curriculum ; with no tastes, literary,
artistic, or scientific, to give zest to life ; residing
in overcrowded and unhealthy lodgings, with little
or no incitement or incentive to virtuous living,
such as the Church supplies in even the very worst
districts of London—one or two filthy and tumble-
down temples being the only outward evidence of
religion ! Set them, lastly, in an environment such
as we have alluded to, with temptations brought to
their very doors, and then perhaps we may have
some sort of imaginable parallel to the condition of

things which we have been, through half a century
of hopelessly misdirected educational activity, so
assiduously creating for ourselves; though for an
actual one we should probably have to go back to
the ancient world and the Universities of Rome and
Carthage, as portrayed by Augustine in the fifth
century of our era.

"The Brahmo movement, all credit to it, has
endeavoured to do something to lift the tone of
morals and hold up a purer ideal; but since the
death of its last great leader its influence has been
precarious, and the rival Somajes appear to be in
danger of dying, respectively, of sentimentalism and
metaphysics. The old conservative 'orthodoxy,'
whose practice was in some degree superior to its
principles, and which succeeded in enforcing a certain
amount of domestic restraint upon the members
of the family, has broken up, and the authority
of the overtaxed schoolmaster, intent chiefly upon
his 'passes' and his grant, is obviously no practical
substitute. Christianity, though its influence is
more or less felt, is as yet too far off to be in
direct touch with the moral life of this generation ;
it has been banned by universal Hindu opinion
as a belief the profession of which is criminal and
worthy of excommunication.

"What remedy can be suggested ? A tentative
scheme for the inspection of boarding-houses was
put forward some years back ; but it never came to
the birth, and at best it could but have scratched
the merest surface of the evil. We can see no
remedy but in an appeal to voluntary effort.

" It would surely offer a vocation for many a young layman seeking for some work to do among non-Christian populations, and unable to find any suitable to his particular talents. It is no fanciful appeal we are making, but one that is forced upon us by our own experience. For the sake of the people of India, for the sake of the British Empire, for the sake of morality, for the sake of CHRIST and His FATHER, these things imperatively demand to be done before it is too late!"

The Oxford Mission was ready to do more than condemn—it was prepared to act, and as far as lay in its power to show the way towards at least one line of reform; but it was not until 1894 that they were able to carry their wishes into effect. It was Mr. Douglass who was the chief leader in this enterprise, and to his wisdom and self-sacrifice the success of the hostel, which has now been open for four years, is largely due.

The first step was to find a suitable house, if possible within easy reach of the Mission House. After some search, just what was wanted was found close at hand in a couple of newly-built native houses, which had not been inhabited and which the landlord agreed to throw into one.

The building, as will be seen from the picture, is just of the ordinary native kind, with rooms surrounding an open court in the middle of the house. On the lower floor is the kitchen and students' dining-room. Another room is kept as a common room for the students. This is furnished with a divan running round two sides of the room, with some small tables

and bookcases, which through the kindness of a
Bengali Christian lady and her brother have been
well-filled with books. Another room upstairs was
set apart for Mr. Douglass, who is in charge of the
hostel and who lives there, coming over to the
Mission House for tiffin and dinner, and for the
chapel services. The other ten rooms are occupied
by the students, while the lower room is that of the
Superior. Mr. Douglass, being a Christ Church
man, has termed the hostel the " House,"[1] and the
small bit of ground by its side, enclosed by the
palings, is somewhat euphemistically entitled the
"meadows," which, if they cannot be measured in
acres, are yet big enough for playing Badminton.

With regard to the method on which the hostel
is conducted, it was made clear from the first that
the work was based on Christianity and on that
alone; and every one who applied for a room was
given quite clearly to understand that though no
religious conditions were imposed, such as attending
a Bible-class, and no pressure would in any way be
put upon them, yet the aim of the Mission was
directly and definitely to promote Christianity. It
was wisely determined that no ground should be
given for the charge that the Mission was trying to
gain converts by secondary motives. Every student
has a room to himself, instead of sharing it with
two or three others, as is the custom in the messes;
and none but bona fide students are accepted. They
each pay twelve rupees a month, which is what is

[1] But to this day it is never by the students called anything but the " Douglass Boarding," (1909).

paid in the average lodgings. Of this, nine rupees are returned to them each month for their mess expenses. A Brahman cook is engaged, and the members of the Mission do not go into the dining-room, and thus the rules of caste as regards food are observed. Each student takes it in turn to manage the mess for a month. The " gate," to use a familiar Oxford word, is closed at 9 p.m., and every student is expected to be in by that time, unless he has special leave of absence. As to dis-cipline, it is maintained not by a minute and definite set of rules, but by personal influence and by mutual consent. The rules, in fact, may be summed up in one, which is that those living in the house must behave as gentlemen. The result so far has been quite satisfactory. Mr. Douglass does not accept any applicant without first having a personal inter-view with him, and he reserves to himself the right of dismissing any student. All payments are made monthly; no debts are allowed, nor are students admitted who cannot pay the full fees. The servants are paid by the Mission, and all the furniture is the property of the Mission. At present it has to be subsidized by the committee at home, but there is no reason why it should not be in time self-supporting.[1]

The hostel was opened in June, 1894. It was felt to be a venture, as it was a very strong step for a Hindu to live in the same house with a European, and a still stronger step to live under the immediate influence of a Christian Mission. However, all doubts were quickly removed when some forty applications

[1] As it now is (1909).

BHOOBAN MOHUN SIRCAR'S LANE.

[*To face p.* 88.

were made for the ten rooms which were available;
and not only did the students themselves apply, but
fathers came and entreated Mr. Douglass to take
their sons. So continuous has been the pressure of
applications for rooms that in 1896 the accommodation was doubled by the building of another house
adjoining the hostel, which has now room for twenty-
two students instead of ten, and is quite full.

Thus the hostel, which was started as a venture of
faith, has become an established and, we may hope,
a permanent fact, and is an institution of sufficient
importance to have attracted the favourable notice of
the Government and to figure in an official report.

In 1896 a further enlargement was made, and
accommodation provided for thirty students. This
necessitated having two members of the Mission
resident at the hostel, and afforded the opportunity
for building a small oratory on the roof of the
house, where the daily offices are said and the
Holy Eucharist is celebrated.

An experiment was tried in 1896 by introducing
into the hostel two Christian students, both of whom
were converts. This was perhaps a greater change
than was at first fully realized; but the difficulties,
which for a moment threatened, were happily overcome, and afforded an opportunity of teaching the
other students some useful lessons. What was felt
by the Hindu students at the time may be seen
from the following account, which was written by
Mr. Douglass:

" It was no sooner understood by the Hindu
students what we were doing than we were petitioned

N

against this innovation and violation of their rights. They thought this to be a 'Hindu boarding,' and why were we admitting Christians? We said we looked upon the hostel as a 'Hindu boarding,' and that we should respect caste as hitherto (we've never once set foot in their dining-room), and that the Christian students would, of course, feed apart from the Hindus. Yes, but the Christian students might come into their rooms while they were eating sweets or while the water-jars were there, or they might bathe in their baths! We explained that we had always reserved to ourselves the right to enter any room at any hour of the day or night; that we had bathed in their baths every morning for two years, and that we were Christians. And then they admitted that the Hindus make a very great distinction between a European Christian and a Bengali Christian, and what they are prepared to endure in the former cannot be for one moment tolerated in the latter. This will give you some conception of what a Bengali must be prepared to bear at the hands of his own people on his Baptism. It was then our turn to teach them something of the brotherhood of man in JESUS CHRIST our LORD. It's all quiet now, and we are getting along happily. As far as we can tell at present, the men seem to be a nice lot of fellows; they are certainly a nice-looking lot.

"To us the presence of the two Christians in the hostel makes an enormous difference. That sense of loneliness which but for the fellowship of a very faithful Christian servant would have been sometimes almost intolerable has been almost entirely taken

away. If ever you want to be thrilled through and
through, come and say Prime or Compline with those
two Christian students and the two Christian servants
on the roof of that Hindu boarding-house, over the
heads of those Hindu students whose religion tries
to teach them to think themselves utterly defiled by
so much as the touch of a man who has confessed
JESUS CHRIST."

CHAPTER VI

THE INDUSTRIAL SCHOOL AND VISITS TO PATNA

> " I count life just a stuff
> To try the soul's strength on, educe the man;
> Who keeps one end in mind makes all things serve."

WE must now retrace our steps to the beginning of the year 1893.

This year found the Mission with a staff of nine
priests, one deacon, and several laymen, European
and native. But large though the staff might seem
when compared with that of former years, the great
extension of the work made it none too big; moreover, it was at its full strength for only part of the
year. Mr. Field, who had come for three years, but
who had stayed a fourth in order to help the Mission
over a difficult time, returned in September. Somewhat earlier Mr. Brown and Mr. Franklin left, the
former on a visit to England, while the latter, who
had just been ordained priest, went to gain some
experience in English parochial work before settling
down to the work of the Mission. Mr. Conway
also returned to England to read for a year at
the Theological College at Cuddesdon before his
Ordination.

Though all the work for which the Mission was
responsible could be maintained, it was maintained

under a sense of over-pressure, and there were no means of taking advantage of new openings whenever they offered themselves. Under these circumstances, the work of 1893 was one of quietly carrying on all the various departments of the work—literary, educational, pastoral, and evangelistic—which the Mission had on hand. Only one new development, which was rather the revival of an old part of the work, was undertaken—namely, the forming of an Indian Branch of the Oxford Mission Association, which, first under the secretaryship of Mrs. Cunliffe and afterwards under that of Mrs. Cable, has proved a very real help, not only in collecting funds for the work of the Mission in India, but in drawing together those interested in the Mission, and in gaining new associates. And here we cannot refrain from saying how much the Mission owes, collectively and individually, to the unfailing kindness and sympathy of friends of both nationalities and of all classes, in India, who from time to time have been associated with it.

In 1894 the Rev. Ernest Linwood Strong, of S. John's College, Oxford, who for seven years had been Curate of S. John the Divine, Kennington, joined the Mission, and has since been associated with Mr. Douglass in the care of the hostel, and seems to have very special gifts for work among the students. Another priest, the Rev. R. D. Ringrose, of Merton College, Oxford, and Curate of Wantage, also came with him; but, after a short stay, it was found that the climate of Calcutta was quite unsuited to his constitution; and to his great regret, as well as to the regret of all who knew him, he had to return home.[1]

A visit which took place this year must not pass unrecorded, namely, that of the Rev. Fr. Congreve, of the Society of S. John the Evangelist, Cowley. He very kindly came from Bombay to conduct the annual Retreat for the Brethren of the Epiphany, and he also gave a most attractive lecture to the students on Tennyson's *Palace of Art*, which was one of the text-books for the University B.A. examination for that year.

It may be remembered that we have had cause to mention the Industrial School before in connection with the Oxford Mission High School. This school, which originally belonged to the Society for the Propagation of the Gospel, was started as far back as 1854, and so had, at the period we have now reached, completed its fortieth year. It had been located during its history in various places in or near Calcutta; but in 1887 it at last found a home in a compound and buildings belonging to the Oxford Mission, which were situated just across the road which bounds the property of Bishop's College. It had at that time about fifty boarders, all of whom were Christians. The boys are mostly the sons of Christian villagers living in the Sunderbans, and have come to the Industrial School from the village schools belonging to the S.P.G. Mission in that district. A few of the cleverer lads pass on to the High School at Bishop's College, but the large majority of them are given a good education in

[1] He died September 12, 1908.

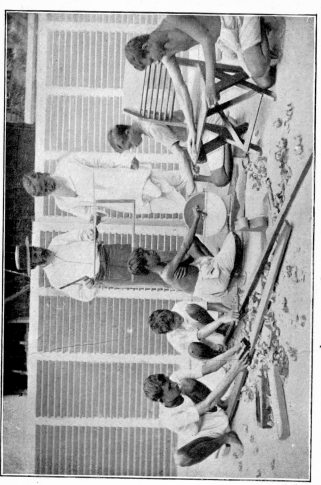

INDUSTRIAL SCHOOL BOYS AT WORK.

[*To face p.* 94.

elementary subjects, and are taught some useful trade. The current expenses of the school are supplied from three sources—from a grant given by the Diocesan Board of Missions, from the fees of the boys, and from the donations and subscriptions (the latter chiefly in the form of scholarships) of friends in India and England. The industrial department of the school, with the exception of a small monthly grant of twenty-five rupees, is entirely self-supporting, and has grown under the care of the headmaster, Rev. M. L. Ghose, into quite a flourishing business, turning out really first-class work.

The importance of such a school is very great, for one of the chief difficulties for native converts is to find employment such as will enable them to earn their living. As a rule a native Christian boy would be refused as an apprentice by any Hindu tradesman or mechanic, and would find it very difficult, even if he knew a trade, to obtain employment under a Hindu master. Consequently the question, " If I become a Christian, how shall I support my family ? " is a very serious one ; while native Christians who have no means of earning their own living become often little more than pensioners of some mission, and as a natural result of such a condition frequently bring reproach upon Christianity. There is, then, a very great need of industrial schools, and of industrial businesses employing native Christians, and managed on really business principles. Printing, weaving, oil-crushing, carpentering, blacksmith and engineering work all offer suitable openings, provided they are

taken up and managed by men who really understand the work.   There is no reason that the
managers should be missionaries in the technical
sense of the word, but they should be really
Christian men, who would undertake such work in
the ordinary business way, but with the aim of
employing only Christian workmen.   This has, in
fact, been tried by a printing firm in Bombay,
which is now largely an industry for native
Christians; and it is worthy of note that when,
during the plague, many of the business houses
had to be closed because the workmen had fled,
this firm was able to remain open, as not one
of the native Christian employés left them.   As
a step towards this, and a very important step,
the Industrial School claims a place, and each year
it gives increasing evidence of its great usefulness,
both as a school in the ordinary sense and as
a school of technical instruction.

Since 1887, when the school moved to its present
position close to Bishop's College, it has been
steadily growing in numbers, until from a total of
fifty boys in 1886 it had risen in 1894 to a hundred
and ten.   This made it absolutely necessary to
provide new buildings.   It was resolved to build
an entirely new school, with a chapel, dining-hall,
large dormitories, and masters' rooms.   The work
was begun in this year, and finished in 1896, at a
cost of £2,000.   A considerable amount was saved
by the care of the Rev. M. L. Ghose and the
staff of the Industrial School, who superintended
the work and had the woodwork made in the

school itself. The new building has not only provided an adequate and commodious home for a hundred and sixty boys, but it has enabled the old buildings which were scattered about the compound to be pulled down, and thus has given ample room for the erection of new and better workshops.

In the beginning of 1895 the industrial department was affiliated to the Government Engineering College at Seebpoor, near Calcutta, and three of the boys attended the college as day scholars. This was an important step, as it gave an opportunity to the boys of learning the higher branches of engineering and carpenters' work, as well as the making of models and framing estimates. It also enabled the school to buy tools at cost price, and has been the means of its adding instruction in blacksmiths' and other ironwork to that of carpentering. Finally, by an arrangement the details of which need not be explained, it was agreed that the Oxford Mission should permanently take over the Industrial School, for which it had, as we have seen, provided entirely new buildings, and should in exchange hand over to the Society for the Propagation of the Gospel the old Oxford Mission High School, which, since 1886, had been housed in Bishop's College compound and in buildings belonging to the Society. The Mission thus possesses a school of which it may well be proud, and which is a most valuable contribution on the part of the Oxford Mission to that most important work of building up the native Christian community.

o

But to return to the Mission House and the work
which flows more directly from it.   It will be remembered that we have alluded once or twice to visits
which were made by members of the Mission from
time to time to Patna and Dacca, both large towns
in the Bengal Presidency, in each of which there are
colleges with a considerable number of students.   It
is much to be wished that the Mission were strong
enough to have a permanent branch house at least at
Patna, but till the staff is considerably increased that
is impossible.   That the Brethren very much desire
to take up this work is shown in a letter written by
a member of the Mission in this year on this very
point.   He says :

" It is somewhat disheartening to be so often prevented in doing work which needs very much to be
done, and which ought to be done by the Oxford
Mission.   Calcutta is the centre to which all students
from the rest of the Presidency eventually come, and
it would be a great advantage to have had touch
with them before they get absorbed in a great mass
of Calcutta students.   The atmosphere of Calcutta is
not congenial to honest inquiry, and seems, I believe,
to get less so than it was when the Mission first
came here, twelve or thirteen years ago.   This is
due, perhaps, partly to a wave of anti-European
feeling which seems to be passing over Calcutta just
now, and partly to a revival of philosophic Hinduism.
These difficulties are less felt in the country districts ;
and the students in the country colleges are, I think,
much more open to the appeal of religion than those
here in Calcutta.

" Also visits of the kind I am speaking of might have another and very important result—namely the establishment of schools for Hindu boys, managed by Christian masters. A good school is almost certain to get abundance of pupils, and very much might be done, if not in the way of actual conversion (which in the case of boys still under their parents' control would not be practicable or desirable, except in very exceptional cases), yet in the way of raising the boys to a higher moral level and giving them a conception of moral responsibility. If that could be done, as it might be, through schools managed by Christian masters, it would be making a very real preparation for the acceptance of the Christian Faith in later life ; for where we are now so constantly baffled is in the fact that with the greater number of inquirers one has to go back to the very first principles, and we constantly lose sight of them before we have time to get any further."

Occasional visits are therefore all that, at present, the Mission can manage. In February Mr. Brown and the Superior went to Patna, the capital of Behar and a large centre of education. They hired a small house in the bazaar, established themselves in the midst of the people, and then announced that they were at home to visitors. They began with some lectures in the hall of a Hindu college, which was kindly lent to them by the proprietor. These were attended by crowded audiences, and they served as a useful mode of introduction to the people. At first visitors were rather slow in coming, but after a time they conquered their shyness and came in a constant stream.

One incident is characteristic.   Mr. Brown and the
Superior were sitting at breakfast one morning after
a lecture given on the previous evening by Mr. Brown
on " Ideals of Life."   A Hindu youth of about sixteen entered, abruptly remarking, " I want some
higher ideals of life."   They asked him to sit down
in an adjoining room till breakfast was over.   Then
Mr. Brown went to him, and as a preliminary began
to read and explain the Ten Commandments, when
the youthful idealist interrupted him with the remark,
" Oh, I have written a book on the Ten Commandments, and made ten more of my own ! "   However,
other visitors were of a more promising kind, and
with some they had very interesting conversations.
After a few days the Superior had to go back to
Calcutta, and Mr. Ringrose came up to supply his
place.   He and Mr. Brown stayed about a fortnight,
and ended their visit with a series of magic-lantern
lectures, on the life of our LORD, in the courtyard of
their house.   Crowded audiences came each night,
and seemed much interested.

In March, Mr. Brown and Mr. Walker paid a visit
to Dacca, the largest educational centre in Bengal
next to Calcutta.   They had a series of lectures,
which were fairly successful ; but on the whole they
were not so favourably impressed with the students
at Dacca as with those at Patna.   Mr. Brown went
afterwards to Jessore to preside at a students' meeting, and was hospitably entertained by the Baptist
missionary.   It was from Jessore that they received
the curious appeal from some native Christians to
establish a Mission there, on the ground that " there

are no Protestants here, only Baptists and Roman Catholics." Mr. Walker continued the tour, visiting Mymensingh and Comillah, giving lectures in each town; but at the former his lecture was spoilt by a heavy thunderstorm.

That visits such as these were appreciated by the students is shown by the following extract from the *Indian Churchman*, giving an account, from an independent source, of the work done by the members of the Mission at Patna :

" A special interest attaches to the two visits now to be noticed, in that the members of the Brotherhood, like the Apostle of the Gentiles, ' dwelt in their own hired house ' in the city, whence has radiated an influence reaching wider and deeper than can be exercised by the more formal public lectures which were given—powerful and practical as they were. In the choice of subjects for their lectures the special needs and temptations of the large student audiences had been evidently studied, and the crowded hall and verandahs, and the silence and attention of a body usually noisy, was the respectful response to that thoughtfulness.

" There were in all four public lectures, and the mention of their subjects—' Ideals of Life '; ' Student Life in India '; ' Conscience '; ' Life : Its Objects '— shows how appropriate they were. The two lectures on ' Conscience ' and ' Life : Its Objects,' which were not merely sustained oratorical utterances or intellectual feasts, but a masterly combination of philosophic reasoning, practical illustration, and deep, stirring earnestness, held the large audiences at the time of delivery, and have left deep impressions on several.

The close of 1895 brought a most welcome addition to the staff at Bishop's College in the person of the Rev. W. L. Nanson. It had for some time been apparent that the burden of the double responsibility of the college and the Oxford Mission, not to mention a vast amount of diocesan and other work which fell upon Mr. Whitehead, was more than one man could rightly bear. This was now becoming a still more pressing matter, as not only was the work of the Oxford Mission increasing, but there was a prospect of a new and very heavy charge coming upon them in the immediate future ; while the work of the college had largely increased, and plans were being considered for practically doubling the number of students. Fortunately, at this time Mr. Nanson, who had for some years been in charge of the Mission belonging to the Cowley Fathers, at Poona, on account of the Fathers being able to increase their staff in India, felt free to resign his charge there and accept the post at Bishop's College which Mr. Whitehead offered to him. In him the college gained a missionary of tried experience and of great capacity, and his appointment was not only a real addition to the strength of the college, but was a joy to the members of the Oxford Mission, to many of whom he was personally known.

In December, 1896, Mr. Conway and Mr. Franklin both returned with the Superior, who had been on a visit to England, and brought with them two new members for the Mission—the Rev. Charles Thomas

Campion, late scholar of Oriel College, Oxford, Curate of S. Ann's, Manchester, and the Rev. John Roper Cooke, late scholar of Wadham, Curate of Downham, in the Diocese of Ely. Unfortunately, Mr. Campion was attacked with fever soon after his arrival, which clung to him with such persistence that he was obliged under the doctor's orders to give up the hope of remaining in India.

A third member who joined the Mission this year was Mr. Barber, a layman. He was an old friend of the Oxford Mission, and had been in business in Calcutta. For some time he had been much drawn to more direct missionary work, and in the early part of 1896 he resigned his post in the firm in which he was working, and offered himself as a lay-brother to the Mission. His help was especially valuable not only as affording a witness to the fact that English laymen are keen in the cause of missions, and because he brought his business capacities to the service of the Mission, but chiefly because through his past connection with the business firms in Calcutta he brought the Mission into touch with a class of educated Bengalis which it had never reached before ; namely, what are known as the office Babus—that is, clerks engaged in mercantile and other offices. These are generally men of maturer age and character than the average student, and many of them being the parents of lads who were at college, the link which was thus formed between them and the Mission was a valuable one.

CHAPTER VII

THE BARISAL MISSIONS

" What, my soul! see thus far, no further, when doors great
and small,
Nine and ninety, flew ope at one touch, should the
hundredth appal?
In least things have faith, yet distrust in the greatest
of all? "

IT was well that this accession of strength came
when it did, for a new and very important
sphere of work came into view towards the end of
1895 under circumstances which made it impossible
for the Mission to refuse to accept it. This was
the care of the S.P.G. Missions in a large country
district in Eastern Bengal, known as the district of
Barisal. The reasons which led to the acceptance
of this work by the Oxford Mission were given by
the Superior in the annual report of 1895, from which
we quote the following statement:

" More than fifty years ago a Baptist Mission
was established there (i.e., in the district of Barisal)
and a considerable number of converts made. In
1848 one of the Baptist preachers separated from
them upon a question of discipline, and was followed
by a large number of his converts. In 1864, after
repeated applications, the separatist body was
received into the Church of England by Bishop

Cotton, and in 1872 their leader, Mr. Bareiro, was ordained deacon by Bishop Milman. In 1879 Mr. Bareiro died, and the Society for the Propagation of the Gospel decided not to carry on the work, believing that Mr. Bareiro's following had practically died out. This, however, was not the case, and those of his followers who remained were absorbed by the Baptists. One result was that many of them were required to be re-baptized. This they strongly objected to. Some resisted for three, four, or five years, and some held out for fifteen years till the Church of England came back to them. Then the children were not baptized, and this was a grievance which, apart from any theological knowledge, wounded the feelings of many who wished their children admitted into the fold of CHRIST.

" However, it is probable that no movement would have been made but for difficulties which arose among the Baptists themselves. The result was disorganization and dissatisfaction all over the district. The pastoral work was made self-supporting by being practically abolished. When travelling in the district I found large congregations of some three or four hundred Christians under the pastoral charge of men who could hardly read or write. This stirred up a feeling of opposition, and led the former members of the Church of England to claim once more their privileges as Churchmen. In 1892 a petition was sent to the Bishop of Calcutta, numerously signed, which stated that a considerable number of Christians in the district belonged to the Church of England, and had been compelled to join the Baptists against their will, and that they earnestly desired to have their children baptized and have the services of their own Church.   This was followed by other similar petitions, till at last, in 1894, the Bishop sent me into the district to inquire into the matter, with the result that at the beginning of this year (1895) it was resolved by the Bishop, with the full consent of the Board of Missions, to receive back these people and establish schools and services for them in the various villages.   I visited the district myself in March, and stayed there for about three weeks. Mr. Brown spent nearly a month there in July, and I was there again for five weeks in September and October.   As the result of a year's work there, there are now about a thousand members of the Church of England in the district.

"During my last visit I baptized over one hundred and ninety persons of all ages, from eighty years to eight days, and received into the Church of England over one hundred and sixty men and women."

The result of the past deplorable desertion of her children by the Church is touchingly shown in an incident which came to the notice of Mr. Whitehead in the course of his tour in the district, of which he wrote as follows :

"The old reader of the Mission in Potihar, in spite of what might well seem irresistible temptations to abandon the Church of his Baptism, was more faithful to her than she was to him.   For fifteen years he has remained steadfast with his

[*To face p.* 106.]

BOATS ON THE RIVER NEAR BARISAL.

family, and has kept two other men faithful with him, one an old man of seventy-four years of age, and another a man of about forty with his wife and child. The old reader has a son of about thirty-five with a wife and two children at Potihar, and a younger son now studying medicine at Barisal. It is a melancholy commentary on the slackness with which the work was carried on twenty or thirty years ago that, with the exception of the old reader himself and his wife, not a single one of these believers in CHRIST and faithful adherents of the Church had ever been baptized. By the help of a tattered Prayer Book and Bible the old man has during these fifteen years kept alive the seed of faith and hope in the hearts of this small flock in the wilderness. But, apart from his ministrations, they had been absolutely destitute of all means of grace. He and his wife had not received the Holy Communion for all those years, and their children and grandchildren had grown up untaught and unbaptized. It may well be imagined that our coming was to them all like the sight of a sail to shipwrecked sailors on a desert isle, and was felt as a direct answer to their prayers and longings."

At another village, when Mr. Whitehead asked the Christians there whether they wished to return to the Church, they made the pertinent reply that they had never left it! They wanted, rather, the Church to return to them. It is surely, then, a cause for great thankfulness that it has been given to the Oxford Mission to remove this reproach

from the Church in Bengal which has lain upon
her for fifteen years, and to bring again her Faith,
her Sacraments and discipline to the children she has
used so ill.

To one who is familiar with Church work in
English country districts the work in Barisal presents, at least outwardly, a great contrast, but a
contrast which has its own special attractions. It
is a work which exerts over all who enter on it
a strange fascination, kindling in them a deep love
for the poor, simple, patient souls who, in their
poverty and loneliness, and in much ignorance, and
with many moral failings, are yet bearing witness,
sometimes with startling and beautiful fidelity, to
the Faith of JESUS CHRIST in the midst of a vast
heathen population. In the hope that it may
kindle the desire in the hearts of some who read
it to offer themselves to the Mission for this work
we feel constrained to reprint the following deeply
interesting account by Mr. Brown of one of the tours
made in the district.

"A land of slow, sad rivers—an unfinished land,
which looks as though only yesterday the fiat had
gone forth, 'Let the waters under the heaven be
gathered together unto one place, and let the
dry land appear.' A few miles further south,
indeed, it gives up the attempt to call itself *dry*
land at all, and confesses itself to be mere slimy,
muddy jungle, abandoned to the crocodile and
the tiger. Further to the north, where I am going,
it is still the normal condition of the country to be
under water for the greater part of the year: such is

the nature of this vast delta of the Ganges—a triangle whose base from Chittagong on the east to Calcutta on the west covers some two hundred and fifty miles, and which only at its northern apex reaches a consistency where you can be sure of your footing all the year round.

"And yet it is a wonderful country in one respect, and that is in the richness of its soil. It is like Egypt after a full Nile. It supports an immense semi-aquatic population. Here they come, tumbling about amongst the rice-fields, all the little children running to see the daily wonder of the steamer, splashing and dancing with delight in their mother-nakedness as it sends up a wave for them to roll about in. Such sweet little wistful faces! At first I try to look at each one and think of the life that lies before him—the long, patient labour of the fields, like those men one sees yonder planting out their rice with the water up above their waists—the small modicum of knowledge that will come to him, and then his eternal destiny. One by one I look into their faces; but now they come crowding too thick for me to do this any more. I am told that this small division of the district contains two-and-a-half millions of people. I seem to have seen almost that number to-day, and one's brain sinks back bewildered and fatigued at the thought of them all, till I recall that beautiful saying, 'Only the Infinite Pity is equal to the infinite pathos of human life.' Perhaps such a day of idleness and dreams is not the worst preparation for a spell of missionary work.

"Arrived at Barisal, I was taken in by our good

friend the magistrate—a faithful son of the Church,
whose spiritual eye is not dimmed by residence
amongst the heathen or by the fewness of his
opportunities for divine worship. There is always
something very touching in ministering to the ' two
or three' who gather together in these out-of-the-way
Indian stations for their rare privilege of receiving
the Bread of Life, and the Sunday here was consequently a bright one. On Monday we were to
plunge into the unknown. I found that a huge
house-boat, of something very like the well-known
Thames build, had been provided for me and my
expected companion; but as he did not turn up,
I should have had it all to myself had not a
Christian named Jogendra Chandra Chakravarti
volunteered to accompany me—' faithful Jogen,' as
I soon learnt to call him, for he looked after all
my wants with the greatest kindness and care.
With us was a cook, an unkempt native of Barisal,
and the boat was manned by a *manji* and seven
mallahs—all Mussulmans—with whom I became very
friendly in the course of the voyage.

" Barisal is the centre of a large district, and is
thronged with schoolboys and college students, and
one does not escape from them without a lecture.
' We want to hear something for our moral improvement' is the form in which the request comes. So
after the inevitable lecture and dinner, I was ready
about 9 p.m. to make a start in our comfortable boat,
it being arranged that we should travel all night.
That being the case, I was not surprised when I
awoke some time in the small hours of the morning

to find that the boat was at anchor, and we had come only a mile or two. The *manji* of course had an excellent excuse, and it was not till daylight that we really got under way, thus reaching Wuzeerpore at midday instead of in the early morning. Here we had our first and only accident. The wind and the current together caught the boat as it was trying to get into a certain creek, and the huge monster swung with considerable force against the bank. A crash, a groan, a noise of broken glass, and I rushed into the cabin to see what had happened. There I saw a heap of things on the floor, sprinkled here and there with dabs of blood, and amidst them the poor cook curled up into a very forlorn-looking bundle. However, on investigation, things did not prove so bad as they looked. The crash had only meant the breaking of one small pane of glass; the blood was from the cook's nose, which had come into contact with the glass, but had not sustained any very serious injury; and the net result was only to give him rather more of a brigandish appearance than before. He was, however, very sorry for himself, and indulged in fever for the next few days.

" From Wuzeerpore to Dhamsar, our first village, is only about four miles, but those four miles were not easy to accomplish, since the rains were late this year, and the fields were too wet to walk over, and yet not wet enough in all places for a boat. So, leaving the big boat behind me, I got into a smaller one, in which we accomplished about three-quarters of the journey, and then were met by Alok Sircar the poet, with a still smaller boat, into which I was transferred. It was propelled by his son, Shitol, a nice, bright-looking lad of about sixteen. In this boat it was necessary to sit tight and not cough or sneeze, if you did not want to find yourself struggling in the water amongst the long stalks of the rice plants, through which we were making our way. The water got more and more shallow, and Shitol had sometimes to get out and push the boat over a ridge, but they would not hear of my doing the same. Soon we came upon little Gopal, his brother, with eyes like a startled fawn, plunging hip-deep into the water to get to school; and at last the boat had to give up the attempt to make any further progress, and the journey had to be finished by all of us wading through the mud.

"At Dhamsar we were received by Chandra, the catechist of the whole district, and the chief leader of the movement which has compelled us to take up this work. He is a most thoughtful, earnest man, and as he accompanied me on the journey every day I felt an increasing affection and respect for him. For many years he has been working his way towards the Church of England, having been much helped by his great friend, the French Roman Catholic priest, who lives at a neighbouring village; and this year, after instruction from Mr. Whitehead, he was confirmed by the Bishop. The story of the return of these people to the Church has been already told, and I need not allude to it any more, except to say that, having started with the feeling that it is a great pity, if it can possibly be avoided, for two bodies of

Christians to be working in the same field, I came to
the conclusion before the end that we should have
been doing a great wrong if we had refused to come
to the aid of these members of our Church. The
Baptists are naturally rather sore; but, after all, the
people are not 'their people' nor 'our people,' as
missionaries are apt rather unwarrantably to suppose,
but have their own conscientious convictions, which
must be respected; and certainly there are many
who feel that the Baptism of their children, and
Confirmation, are privileges which they have a right
to claim. Enough, perhaps, has been said of the
abandonment fifteen years ago of some three thousand members of our Church, leaving them no choice
between remaining without any Christian services
at all and joining the Baptists. Of these three
thousand, I heard in one place of two hundred and
fifty, and in another of three hundred, on whom this
policy had the effect of sending them back to Hinduism, and probably one-fourth of the whole number
are in this condition. This is the saddest part of the
whole matter, and I have not hitherto succeeded in
tracing any of these people.

"At Dhamsar we had services in the open air, as
the church is not yet built. One inconvenience of
this is that in the morning the sun is apt to get hot
before you have finished, and in the evening it is
necessary to seize the psychological moment between
the heat of the afternoon and the approach of darkness, while at this time of the year the rain is always
liable to disconcert your arrangements. However,
the people are wonderfully patient and good-tem-

2

pered, and all these little difficulties are easily got over. On this and subsequent visits I learnt greatly to love many of these Dhamsar people. At Christmas I spent a week with them—the best house, made of mud and mats, being given up to me ; and if I had been a king in his palace I could not have been treated more royally. I brought a box full of little presents for the children—balls, knives, dolls, etc. They had never seen such things, and were lost in astonishment and delight. Amongst other things was a Jack-in-the-box with a hideous black face—value about sixpence. The fame of it spread far and wide, and a Hindu woman from a neighbouring village made a journey, as she said, ‘ to see Ketu.’ Now, Ketu is a monster of Hindu mythology, who swallows up the sun and the moon, and I should not be surprised to find that Jack-in-the-box enshrined in a temple and worshipped on my next visit.

“ One effect of the moisture of the climate is that the children begin to smoke almost from the cradle. At a village called Narikelbari—‘ the House of the Cocoa-nut ’—the following dialogue took place between myself and a small urchin of five : ‘ Have you had your morning pipe ? ’ ‘ I have.’ ‘ How long have you been a smoker ? ’ ‘ Oh, for years ! ’

“ Their occasional excursions into the Bible in search of names for their children have often a touch of genius about them. A family of four boys were called Samson, Jonah (pronounced Junus), ‘ Paulus,’ and then—as though all Jewish and Christian literature had been exhausted—they fell

back on the Hindu Ganesh. This, however, is out-
done by a family in the Sunderbans, where the boys
are called Benjamin—the eldest—Reuben, Judah,
and Herod! Others like to combine the law, the
prophets, and the gospel : thus three brothers were
called Paul, Gershom, and Micah, and a boy in
another family rejoiced in the names of Seth Titus.
As a rule, however, they are satisfied with such
names as are borne by Hindus, in spite of their
heathenish associations ; and in this, I think, they
are justified by New Testament precedent.

"At the evening service I gave an instruction in
Bengali. Here my pride received a great blow. I
asked Chandra whether the people had understood
me. 'Yes,' he said, 'they understood you—because
the people *here* are accustomed to Englishmen's
Bengali.' After that I thought he had better inter-
pret for me. After service they entertained us with
the *Pilgrim's Progress*, a sort of 'oratorio' founded
on Bunyan's great allegory. These *játras*, as they
are called, are very popular among the people, being
a form of religious entertainment quite indigenous to
Hinduism. A party will often make a vow to sing
through the whole of the *Ramayan* or *Mahabharata*
—the great Hindu epics ; and the performance takes
several weeks. The *Pilgrim's Progress* did not take
several weeks, but it took a good many more hours
than I could keep awake for. By midnight they had
only got as far as the Slough of Despond, which
'Christian' thought a very good place in which to
have a quiet smoke of the favourite 'hubble-bubble'
or *hookah*. The boys sang as though they would

split their throats. The whole composition has been versified by Alok Sircar, one of our old Church people, and his four sons are the chief musicians— Bihari, Shitol, Gopal, and Nipal.

" I must tell you a little story about Gopal, a dear little boy of about ten. It will illustrate how among these Christians of the second or third generation the conscience can become tenderly sensitive, whereas amongst Hindus, such is the baneful effect of the caste system, our great difficulty is to discover whether they have any conscience at all. On one of my visits I missed a small toy from my box, and discovered that it had been carried off by Gopal's youngest brother, an infant too small to be responsible for the theft. I sent Shitol to say that it must be given back, and that he must teach his little brother not to steal. Shitol, however, misunderstood me and gave the message to Gopal. Presently there came back to me not only the toy in question, but everything I had ever given to Gopal—a picture or two, a knife, one or two toys—precious things, which had evidently been fondly treasured. Not knowing of the mistake, I was at a loss to understand this, and sent for Gopal to explain. For a long time he stood by me silently weeping, unable to speak; at last it came out, amid many sobs, that he had been accused of the theft, and, deeply wounded by such a suspicion, had determined to surrender all his treasures. Of course the matter was cleared up, and with some difficulty I was able to restore his peace of mind and persuade him to take back his property.

WOMAN CARRYING WATERPOT AND CHILD.

[To face p. 117.

"From Dhamsar we went to Morakhati, examined the school, and held a service with the Christians. A Hindu boy named Rojoni made great friends with me, and his father, Fedoo, brought a very acceptable offering of milk. We often get presents from the Christians, but it is rare for Hindus to bring us anything, and I appreciated the courtesy accordingly. Thence, through a beautiful shaded glen, where broad plantain-leaves spread their shade, undamaged by the wind which so often cuts them into strips, to Potihar, where we found the old reader, Mohan Modon, a full account of whom appeared in Mr. Whitehead's first letter from Barisal. This is the only place where the Roman Catholics are working alongside of us, they having, with the greatest courtesy, yielded to the wish of our own people to return to us. Potihar is a small place, with but a few Christian families, only one of whom is of our Church, and, but for the good old reader, whom we cannot desert, we should hardly think it necessary to keep up a station there. It is a great comfort to me to feel that our coming has not multiplied the divisions among the Christians in the district, for, whereas before there were Roman Catholics and Baptists, there are now practically only the Baptists and ourselves. The Romanists have never done very much here, and they will now, I think, concentrate their work in one or two places which lie quite out of our track.

"Dhandoba, the next place, is the old headquarters of the Mission. Here is a noble old man, Dhononjoy, bent nearly double with age, who for fifteen years resisted all solicitations to be rebaptized, and has lived to welcome back his own Church. On my first visit here I could only find two children who could say the LORD'S Prayer, but when I went again at Easter, six months later, I found a splendid school of eighty children, even the tiniest of whom could repeat the LORD'S Prayer and the Creed, and many of them were well instructed in the Catechism, besides secular learning. There were also some bright Mussulman lads, who petitioned me that they might be allowed to have some Christian instruction given to them. All this is the work of my ' faithful Jogen' and another man, named Hira Lal Sircar, who have worked here with the greatest possible zeal and diligence. Our plan is to let all who will come to the school, whether Christians or not, but not to give religious instruction to the non-Christians unless they ask for it. In many cases they do ask for it, as here, and then I feel sure it is received with a much better grace than if it were forced down their throats. There are many hopeful Hindu boys in the schools; at Shuagram one of them, fourteen years old, has wrung from his reluctant parents their consent to his being baptized, and I hope to baptize him on my next visit.

" Near Dhandoba is the Hindu village or small town of Goela, where our huge boat had to stay while we went in a smaller boat to Dhandoba. One day I was rather unwell, and had to stay at home with the boat while Chandra went to the Christians to prepare them for my coming the next day. Here the *manji* (the Mussulman boatman) made a brilliant

suggestion.   He said : ' Sahib, why should you
trouble yourself to go all round the district in this
way ?   Let us keep the boat here, and you stay in
it, and send the Babu (Chandra) to do the work '—a
suggestion very characteristic of India.   Our next
halt was at a village called Torun Sen.   Here the
good French father has sold his chapel to us, and let
his people depart with his blessing.   He appears to
have solved for himself in our favour the question
which has so long been agitating the authorities at
Rome.   ' The Church of England '—so his words
have been reported to me by the people—' is not far
from the truth.   They have fourteen annas to the
rupee, whereas the Baptists have only one anna.'
' But we say,' added my informants, ' that the Church
of England has sixteen annas and the Roman Church
fourteen.'   At this place there was a Hindu to be
baptized—three had been preparing, but two of them
held back at the last moment.   On our way to the
place an old lady came up to us in a boat, and asked
whether we had seen her ' child,' who, she had heard,
was going to join the Christians.   I entered into a
conversation with her, urging her to come too, and
offered her some fruit, which she rejected with great
disdain, thinking that I wanted to bribe her.   To my
great amusement, the Mussulman *manji* came to our
assistance.   His exhortation was a very simple one :
' Give up worshipping *Saitan*,' said he, ' and worship
CHRIST.'   This too, however, failed in its effect.
(When I asked the *manji* afterwards whether he
would worship CHRIST, he wanted to know whether
it would mean giving up Mohammed.)   Arrived at

Torun Sen, the Christians collected, the old lady's 'child' appeared—a strong-looking man of about thirty—and I began the Baptismal Service. In the middle of it there was a whoop and a yell, and a figure threw itself flat upon the ground in front of me, straight as a tree falls, and began banging its head against the floor. It was the old lady herself whom I had seen in the boat. She was, I believe, trying to kill herself; but fortunately the mud floor was newly made, and she did not do her head much harm. She, however, made such a noise that it was impossible to proceed with the service, so I suggested that we should adjourn to the tank, where the Baptism was to take place. We both went down into the water, but three times the old mother flung her arms round her son's neck and succeeded by main force in dragging him up the bank. It was a singular scene, blended of tragedy and comedy. Beneath her eccentric way of expressing herself was the heart-breaking sorrow of a mother who felt that her son was being lost to her for ever. The man behaved with wonderful patience, and only at the last shook her off a little roughly. She lay moaning on the ground; and the Hindus present, who mostly seemed to be on our side, prevented her from interrupting the service any more. One of them said to me afterwards, 'We are all coming soon.' We then went down into the water once more, and I asked the man whether he was quite firm in wishing to be baptized then. He said he was, and answered the questions in the service calmly and distinctly; so I baptized him. I have seen him several times since, and he remains steady. He was married this year by Mr. Whitehead to a Christian widow—another blow, I fear, to his mother, to whom, as a Hindu, widow marriage is an abomination. She does not at present show any sign of following his example, but I trust we may yet see the fruit of the many prayers which have been offered for her.

"With a fresh breeze and a glowing sky we sailed away that evening over the apparently solid land of the rice-fields into the northern division of the district, which is under a different reader, Shashadar Chakravarti by name. He is a much younger man than Chandra, and has not the same ripeness of judgement; but he has an abundant supply of energy, a quality which is not always prominent in our Bengali Mission workers. Our first halt was at his own village, Shuagram, where we found his gentle and courteous old father, so graphically described in Mr. Whitehead's letter. The boat came to anchor in the garden, and in the narrow space between it and the house we had to have our service, no church having been yet built. For Baptism it was very convenient, as we had only to go down a few steps into the water. We always baptize by immersion, both to avoid ' offence ' to the Baptists and because there really seems no reason why in India this, the primary intention of the Church, should not be observed. This district is much more compact than the southern one, there being twelve villages within a radius of about six miles. Consequently the time occupied in getting about with our lumbering old house-boat was not so long,

R

and I was able to see more of the people. On my second visit, after the Bishop had held his Confirmation at the beginning of this year, we had one hundred and thirty - eight communicants, which, with eighty-one in the other district, makes two hundred and nineteen. There must be nearly as many more waiting to be confirmed, and the total number of Church people is about two thousand. At one place where I went I was told there were a number of former members of the Church who had not yet come back. When I asked them what they were going to do, they said, with a charming frankness, 'We are going to wait and see whether you will deceive us again.' At Pakhor an old man died a few months ago, saying he was very sorry he had not lived to see his own Church re-established in the country. His widow and children were among those whom I baptized.

"Our present great want is that of churches and schools. These are of very simple construction, in most places being made only of mats; but the question is complicated by the fact that in this part of the district if any one wants to build a house, he first has to build an island to put it on. This about doubles the expense.

"The last place which I visited was Kolligram, an outlying village which it took us one and a half days to get to by boat. On our way we caught a great number of tortoises. When I say 'we,' my part consisted in looking on from the boat, while one of the men, who was very clever at it, ran along the bank, and whenever he saw a tortoise sitting near the water made a jump for it. The tortoise jumped at the same time; but in two cases out of three he would catch it in his hands before it could dive to the bottom. They are eight or ten inches in length, and are said to be very good eating, but in common with the pig are abhorred by Mussulmans (*Lev.* xi. 29), though Hindus eat them. Kolligram is a large place, where we have some two hundred Christians. I found them keeping school under a tree, and assembling for worship in the very narrow space supplied by the verandah of a mud house. At this distant village only seven people have been confirmed, but they all came to Holy Communion, after we had had a searching preparatory service the day before. This, indeed, was the chief object of my tour, to admit those who had been confirmed to their first Communion ; and none were allowed to communicate unless they had gone through a preparation as careful as it was possible to make it in the time, including very full questions on the Ten Commandments. They were not expected to make answer publicly, but many touching acknowledgements of sin were made either to me or to the readers, and some quarrels were composed. Altogether I do earnestly hope that the reorganization of the Church here will be of real spiritual benefit to the people, for that can be our only ultimate justification for entering upon a field where so much Christian work has been done before. It distresses me greatly that for some time to come they must be without a resident priest, while we at Calcutta are two or three days' journey from them.

" I must tell you one more story which will illustrate the simple character of this rural Church. While I was at Dhamsar on my last visit, a man came in from a distant village to say that when the Bishop came for the Confirmation in February his steam-launch stuck on a mud-bank just opposite his (the speaker's) house, and he took that as a providential indication that he ought to join the Church of which the Bishop was the head; that he had also had several dreams bearing in the same direction; moreover, that when he went to his own minister to ask him about it, the latter only replied with a Bengali proverb, meaning that where there is something original there will be imitation, and that, going home and thinking over it, he had come to the conclusion that the Church was the original and the Baptists the imitation Finally, what clinched the matter was that eight persons were saved in the Ark, and his family consisted of exactly eight persons. Of course he could not be received on such grounds; but I gave him some instruction, and told him to wait and pray, and it may be that when the Bishop comes again he will be able to fulfil his wish, and receive him into the ark of CHRIST'S Church.

" There are naturally many difficulties and hin- drances, some of which I have hinted at; but on the whole it is a great happiness to work amongst people of such simple faith. Though one can hardly expect them to see it in this light, I feel that the present movement is largely the result of the fidelity with which the Baptist missionaries have done their work, and I pray that we may be able to continue it in such a spirit as to hasten the time when we shall be reunited under one LORD, in one Faith, by one Baptism."

CHAPTER VIII

ANNUS INFAUSTUS

> " Let one more attest—
> I have lived, seen GOD'S hand through a lifetime, and all
> was for best."

THE year on which we are now entering was one
of losses in the organization at home, and of
public anxiety and trouble in India which more or
less affected the Oxford Mission. At the close of
1896 Miss Murray, who for ten years had laboured
with unremitting zeal on behalf of the Mission, was
obliged to resign the office of General Secretary. At
a meeting of the Committee held on December 10th
a resolution was unanimously passed in which the
Committee expressed their high appreciation of her
devoted work, and their deep regret that she felt
herself obliged to resign her charge. Miss Murray's
place was taken by Miss Edith Argles.

In Calcutta, and indeed in all India, 1897 will
long be remembered as an *Annus infaustus*. It
opened with famine and pestilence ; its central
months were marked by earthquake, murder, and
riot, and the cloud of war hung heavy on the north-
west frontier. Of the war, nearly two thousand
miles away, those in Calcutta only heard the echo,
much as we did in England, through the news-

papers. The famine, again, only touched Bengal
lightly, while the plague which was devastating other
parts of India most unexpectedly avoided Calcutta.
But nevertheless the Mission in the person of
Mr. Lloyd had its share in contributing help to the
plague-stricken districts. When the pestilence was
at its height at Bombay, and continual reports came
of the scarcity of nurses in the hospitals, Mr. Lloyd
volunteered to go and do what he could to help the
All Saints' Sisters in their work. His offer was
gladly accepted, and he spent the greater part of
the hot weather and rains on plague duty of various
kinds at Bombay itself and at Kutch Mandvi. His
work in Bombay involved a great deal of night-
nursing under conditions of the most trying kind;
and when the plague decreased there he was sent to
Kutch Mandvi, a town of about twenty thousand
inhabitants, in a native state, on search duty—
searching for cases of plague in the native houses,
accompanied by detachments of Sepoys and police-
men. It was hard work, but to the great joy of the
Mission Mr. Lloyd returned to Calcutta not only
safe and sound, but looking better and stronger for
his labours.

The earthquake and the riots came home to the
Mission more nearly, as they were both felt in their
full force in Calcutta. Of the earthquake a member
of the Mission writes as follows:

"On that memorable Sunday afternoon, June 12th,
I was paying a call in the business part of Calcutta,
when we heard a rumbling, which might have been
that of a very heavy waggon. My host and I

rushed out into the compound. The sight which first struck us was that of a large swinging lamp, swaying backwards and forwards a yard or more in the verandah. Others reported that a similar sight, though inverted, was to be seen wherever there was a tall chimney. 'The massy earth' heaved beneath one's feet as though it had been a ship's deck. This continued for nearly five minutes by the clock. I don't think any of us realized at the time how serious the earthquake was; but when on my way home I passed through some of the principal streets of the city, and saw how there was scarcely a house of any size which had not received some damage, I began to understand that we had undergone an awful calamity. It is said that there are seventy feet of thick mud, which forms a sort of spongy foundation for the whole of Calcutta. This would be a protection against any ordinary earthquake, and no doubt was in great part a protection against this. Nevertheless, that short five minutes had plenty to show for itself. Nearly every church in Calcutta lost a portion at least of its steeple. Very few three-storied houses retained their upper floors intact; houses that were old in nearly all cases lost a part of their walls; in some cases a verandah or a front wall fell into the street bodily, revealing the inner apartments. Yet it would be a great exaggeration to say, as some of the local papers did, that Calcutta was in ruins. Two days after the earthquake one might pass along the street, and except for a house or two under repair, and the truncated condition of the church spires, one could hardly notice any difference. Business on the

Monday, following that Saturday, was in full swing as usual.

"Two instances of real heroism in connection with the earthquake must not pass unnoticed. One was that of the nurses at the hospitals, who, when the buildings were rocking to and fro and were expected every moment to fall, stood by the patients who were unable to leave their beds, encouraging them and cheering them at the risk of their own lives. The Eurasians are often spoken of as a poor race, but we think the heroism of these Eurasian women should not be forgotten. 'I am so sorry I was not in the hospital myself at the time,' was the comment of the Sister who told us of this incident. The other was that of one of the Clewer Sisters, in charge of the European orphanage. All the girls had rushed out; but when they collected in the compound, it was found that one of the teachers was absent, whereupon the brave little Sister ran up all the way to the top of the house, three stories, amidst the crashing of walls and timber, to look for her, only to find that she had slipped out by another way. That, it seems to us, was a deed that deserved the V.C."

The occasion of the riots which took place later in the year, in which Mr. Nanson and Mr. Conway were both injured, though fortunately not seriously so, was the decision of the courts against a man who had squatted on some land which did not belong to him and on which he had built a little shed, which he called a mosque. The claim was as bad in Mohammedan as it was in English law, which was

afterwards acknowledged by the leaders of the
Mohammedan community in Calcutta. Nevertheless, the masses of Mohammedans, who are always
excited by any religious question, became roused,
and there is much evidence to show that the excite-
ment was studiously fanned by a low class of
Mullahs, who are in immediate contact with the
people. The word went forth that no Hindu was
to be attacked, only Europeans and Christians, and
this in spite of the fact that the owner of the land in
question was a Hindu. Consequently, at all street
corners stood men with clubs and stones, vowing
that no European should pass that way without
receiving hurt. There is, however, no proof that
they meant deliberate murder; probably they did
not wish to do more than was necessary to intimi-
date the authorities, though of course no one could
foresee where things would stop when once they
began. Of what followed with regard to the attack
on Mr. Conway and Mr. Nanson we will let Mr. Brown
speak.

" On the evening of the first day a message was
brought that Conway had been attacked and left for
dead in the street. We went out at once to the
place, about a mile from the Mission House, and
there could only learn that he had been seen to be
hit on the head and several other places with stones.
Our next visit was to the neighbouring hospital,
and we found our first grain of comfort when we
learnt from the Sister in charge that nothing had
been seen of him there. We then went back to the
Mission House, passing a second time through the

rioters, who for some reason or other did not attack us. Our hope that he might have got back in our absence was disappointed, and we made our way through the crowd a third time to look for him at S. James's School; and there at last we found him, not much the worse except for a black eye, where he had been hit by a stone, and a sprained knee, which was the result of an old football accident, and had given way again in the tumult. A brick, which had been thrown down upon him from a house, had been warded off by his large pith hat; otherwise he might not have lived to tell the tale. We then got him into our carriage and drove back to the Mission House, being able to avoid the places of danger owing to the advice of a friendly Bengali Babu. Meanwhile, Nanson, at Bishop's College, four miles away, had heard a highly-coloured account of Conway's accident, and drove over at once with a friend, hoping either to rescue him or to give us warning. They were in an open dog-cart, and, as they reached the place where we had passed only a few minutes before, they were saluted with a shower of stones, and arrived at the Mission House bleeding in one or two places, but not seriously hurt. Going back, they fared worse, and for nearly a mile had to run the gauntlet of a mob throwing large stones as hard as they could at the cart, the pony, and themselves. At the end of this they were a mass of cuts and bruises, which laid them up for some days, but fortunately no vital part was injured. The general result of two days' rioting was that some dozen or twenty Europeans were more or less seriously hurt,

but none killed. How many of the rioters were
killed will, I suppose, be never known. The officials
were judiciously reticent, and the bodies were so
speedily disposed of by their companions that probably those who know most about it can only make a
guess. One estimate said seven persons, another
fifteen hundred !

"The worst effect of the whole has been the bitter
feeling it has left behind. The relation between
natives and Europeans is never of the best, and
anything which serves to embitter it is a calamity
to both. As for ourselves, I don't think we have
much to complain of. We scarcely realize how
much we owe to the protection of the English
Government except when that protection is for a
moment suspended. Missionaries in China and
some parts of Africa are face to face with death
every day of their lives. We, on the contrary, have
enjoyed the benefits of the *Pax Britannica* for every
day but two since the Mission was started. Whether
this state of things is as good for the spiritual
interests of our work and of ourselves as a more
precarious condition might be I can hardly say;
certain it is that in temporal matters we could
scarcely be better off than we are."

We have now reached the record of 1898. The
Rev. Charles McLaughlin, of Bishop Hatfield's Hall,
Durham, who went out to join the Mission at the
end of 1897, was a welcome addition to the staff,
though unfortunately it proved no gain numerically,
as Mr. Campion was in the early part of this year
invalided home.

One other departure remains to be chronicled—namely that of Bishop Johnson, who for twenty-two years, as Bishop of Calcutta and Metropolitan of India, has done so much for the organization of the Indian Church on true Catholic principles. This is not the place to dwell upon that work as it affected the Church at large, or on the great and important changes which the Bishop brought about in the twenty-two years of his episcopate. It is of his relation to the Oxford Mission that we have to speak. That relation could not have been happier. It was in response to his call that the Mission was founded. He has looked upon it as his child from the first, and has been its steady friend and wise counsellor through evil report and through good report. No serious step has ever been taken by the Mission without his advice and approval. "Do nothing without the Bishop," has been its consistent policy; and it may safely be said that there is no institution in the diocese, which has been more intimately associated with the episcopate which came to an end in 1898 than the Oxford Mission to Calcutta, and no institution which has greater cause to mourn its termination. Nor was this association between the Bishop and the Mission a merely general one. It was born of the personal interest which he took in every individual member—of the real and unfailing fatherly care and affection with which he watched over, not only their work, but their health, and with which he shared in all their joys and sorrows. This called out on their part a loyal devotion and a reverence and love which were deep and true, and which have made every one who has worked in the Mission feel that, whatever else they may have gained, one thing at least of permanent value has become theirs, "that they have known the Bishop."

It is, perhaps, appropriate that this sketch of the Oxford Mission should close with the episcopate of Bishop Johnson, who under GOD called it into being. Seventeen years is not a long time in the life of an individual, it is still less in the life of an institution ; and yet as we look back over those seventeen years what a great work has been done! Compare the Oxford Mission as it began its work in 1881 and as it presents itself to us in 1898. It started in a hired house, with a staff of three priests, strange to the work, to the language, to the country, and to the people ; it has to-day a magnificent house of its own, standing in the very centre of the native and student quarter of the city, with a staff of nine priests[1] and two laymen, numbering among them men who have gained not only an intimate knowledge of the chief missionary problems with which the Church has to deal in Bengal, but also a close and deep sympathy with the people among whom they work, and a real grasp of the many religious and philosophical problems which are presented by modern Hinduism.

They have, again, gathered round them a large and increasing band of loyal and devoted Bengali

[1] This number was, through the recent appointment of Mr. Whitehead to the See of Madras, the return of Mr. McLaughlin to England, and the illness of Mr. Conway, soon practically reduced to six.

priests, catechists, and schoolmasters, as well as
scholars and students ; not "agents," as some missionary bodies so mistakenly term them, but fellow-
workers in the highest and truest sense, men knit to
the Mission and the college by the closest ties of
common worship, common sympathy and aim, and
common love. Through them and with them the
Oxford Mission has enormously raised the standard
of spiritual life among the native Christian congregations in Calcutta. This alone would have justified
its existence when it is remembered that, in the
opinion of all competent observers, the conversion
of India as a whole will depend much more upon
the native ministry than upon European Missions ;
though these for a long time will be absolutely
necessary to support and organize the work of the
native Church. They have, further, established a
complete system of education, starting from the
primitive village schools in the country districts and
mounting by successive and connected steps through
the Industrial School on the one hand to the higher
branches of the mechanical trades, and through the
High School on the other to the degrees of the
Calcutta University : while they have, in connection
with the Society for the Propagation of the Gospel,
their own boarding-schools, their college for resident
students, their theological class, all of which are
entirely filled with native Christians, and for the
most part are housed in ample and well-equipped
buildings.

In the districts of the Sunderbans and Barisal
they have revived large missions which had been

only partially cared for, or altogether neglected, and by persevering labour and firm discipline, and above all by the faithful teaching of the full Catholic Faith, have brought back real Church life to the congregations under their care—a life which is showing itself in continuous growth. By their lectures at the Mission House and by individual intercourse they have year by year been patiently preparing the ground and sowing the seed which, if as yet it has not borne fruit in any large number of conversions, has, it is acknowledged on all sides, had a real influence upon the native society. In the *Epiphany* they have made a paper by means of which they reach a far wider circle than by either lectures or interviews—a paper which has not only an acknowledged position in the eyes of the European and native press of Calcutta, but which is read in many other parts of India, and which is appreciated by friend and foe alike for its ability, its courtesy, and the courage and fairness with which it deals with every question submitted to it. In the hostel they have solved a problem which has baffled the Government and the University of Calcutta; and they have provided an object-lesson as to how the present lamentable condition of the Calcutta students can be improved, as well as created an instrument for missionary work the promise of which each year becomes more sure. Lastly, we venture to say, and we think that many in India would support us in saying it, that by their life and devotion, their earnestness and zeal, their theological and general intellectual ability, and not least by their unswerving loyalty to Catholic Faith and discipline, they have had no small influence on the development and deepening of the life of the Church in India as a whole.

This we claim is a record of work of which even the University of Oxford, with its immemorial traditions and its splendid services to the Faith, may well be proud. For the Oxford Mission, be it remembered, if not officially, yet definitely and distinctly represents Oxford to India. Through it the University of Oxford ministers of her intellectual and spiritual wealth to the deep poverty of the University of Calcutta.

Through the Oxford Mission to Calcutta, and through that heroic and splendid enterprise the Universities' Mission to Central Africa, Oxford is pledged to pay her debt to two great continents. Is that responsibility in any adequate sense realized? Is that pledge in any adequate degree being redeemed? Can we think so when year after year from both Missions comes the pleading cry, often in vain, for more men—a cry which comes from hearts saddened by seeing opportunities lost which only lack of numbers prevents them from accepting?

We have spoken of the position which the Oxford Mission holds in Calcutta and of its influence upon the native society. To what, it may be asked, is this influence to be chiefly attributed? Not, we feel sure, only or chiefly, to intellectual ability, though the Mission contains, and always has contained, men of the highest intellectual culture. Nor, again, do we think that it is due to the fact that they live under a

T

definite if simple form of the religious life—though
such a life has a great attraction for the Hindu,
whose whole mind and nature is profoundly religious.
Nor, once again, is it because they have spoken
smooth things of the religious and moral aspects of
modern Hinduism ; for they have never hesitated
to speak their mind plainly and openly about it.
These things, not excluding the last—for the power
of truthfulness is great even when it goes against
age-long conviction—have no doubt done much ; but
what has given them their real strength has been
that from the first they have shown sympathy to
those among whom they have come to live. It is
known now that every Bengali, be he high caste or
low caste, be he rich or poor, will find a welcome at
the Mission House, will be received with courtesy
and consideration, and will always be sure of a
sympathetic and patient hearing.

The Mission has not fallen into the mistake of
thinking that the Bengali Babu is a paragon of
virtue, or is competent to be entrusted with all and
every form of political responsibility and power.
They have gauged his character much more truly.
But in forming their estimate of him they have
remembered his past history—how he has ever been
the conquered and not the conqueror—how in order
to maintain his own he has had to live by his wits—
and how, as a result, flattery, deception, dishonesty
have been his training for centuries. They have
realized, again, that what he is to-day—half-educated,
with all the faults which imperfect education brings
with it, without any definite belief, and with the

weakening of social and moral restraints which comes from the breaking up of the old before it is replaced by the new—is largely the result of circumstances outside his own control, and which have been in a measure forced upon him—forced upon him by ourselves, who are now his severest critics. For it is to the present system of education, which has been created by the English Government, that the Calcutta Babu owes his existence. This fact alone lays upon England an enormous responsibility towards the educated classes of India.

What has been and is the result of this system on the young educated Bengali we have already shown. It has engaged the anxious attention not only of missionaries, but of every thoughtful administrator in the Indian Government. Whatever the remedies may be which may avert what is at present rapidly becoming a moral disaster, this at least is certain, that there is one essential qualification for all who would successfully touch the problem, and that is sympathy, and not merely criticism. It is just this which in our mind makes the outlook, not only as regards the educated native classes in Calcutta, but as regards our relation to the whole people of India, so anxious.

No one, we think, can have any real knowledge of India without a deep sense of the splendid work which is being done by the great Indian Civil Service, the finest service, we venture to say, which the world has ever seen. This work is recognized by the Indian people; they thoroughly appreciate the benefit of our rule; they are bound to us by

self-interest; they would support us against any
foreign invader; but—and the fact was admitted by
Lord Dufferin himself, than whom few have known
India better—the people do not like us. The reason
is that with all our real desire to do what is right
towards them, with all our real wish and continuous
effort to benefit them, we have not shown sympathy.
As a rule the average Anglo-Indian treats the native
with a discourtesy, we had almost said a rudeness,
which, though it is never openly resented, rankles in
their heart. In the opinion of those who have
known India longest, the separation between the
two societies, English and Indian, grows wider instead of narrower. There are, there must be, many
difficulties. There is always the underlying difficulty
which comes from the relation of a conquered people
to its conquerors. There are, again, all the difficulties which arise from differences of creed and
social customs, and from the enormous dissimilarity
between the mental attitude of the East and of the
West, the very virtues of the one race appearing as
irritating and annoying qualities in the eyes of the
other.

The increasing facilities, again, of intercourse
between England and India which might at first
sight seem to ensure a better understanding between
the two peoples are probably producing the exactly
opposite result. Englishmen do not live in India as
they used to do. It is no longer, as it once was,
practically their home for thirty or forty years. It
is much more now their place of business, from
which they get away on every available opportunity

and as often as they can. This is natural, and we cannot blame them. Again, the exigencies of modern government and the introduction of railways have led to a much more continuous and rapid movement of the government officials from one district to another than in former days; so that the close, intimate, almost paternal relations which used to exist between the rulers and the ruled, each year tend to become less close and less personal. No doubt in many ways the Anglo-Indian has changed for the better, but the fact remains that he is not so near to the people as he formerly was.

It is this nearness, born of personal sympathy, which has been a source of real power to the Oxford Mission. Surely this is worth a great deal, and is a matter which concerns not only the missionary, but every Englishman ; for, after all, the only strong foundation on which any rule can permanently rest is that which is laid on the hearts of the people. We do not minimize the difficulties ; but the old saying still holds true, *Noblesse oblige.* It is because in virtue of our Christian Faith, in virtue of our past heritage—which has made us what we are—that we *are* the greater nation, that we are bound by the very sense of our own greatness to be patient, forbearing, and sympathetic towards those over whom we rule.

CHAPTER IX

CONVERTS

> "A touch divine—
> And the sealed eyeball owns the mystic rod;
> Visibly through His garden walketh GOD."

IT will probably have been noticed that in tracing the history of the Mission no mention has been made of any conversions to Christianity from among the students. This omission we have made purposely, because it seemed best to put together in one place what we desire to say upon this subject.

We will at the outset frankly admit that the number of actual students who have been baptized has been very few. But to any one who understands the conditions of the work in Calcutta this is neither surprising nor discouraging.

There is in the mind of many people at home an impatience at what appears to them an undue slowness in the result of foreign missionary work, though, considering the miserably inadequate and languid way in which the Church of England Missions are supported both as regards men and money, the surprise is, not that they should seem to do so little, but that they should achieve anything at all. As a matter of fact, however, Christianity is spreading in India at a far quicker ratio as regards the population than it spread in Europe in the early days of the Church. It must be remembered also that any really systematic effort at missionary work on the part of the Church in India is scarcely one hundred years old—it would be truer to say, scarcely fifty or sixty years old. Paradoxical as it may appear, it is, we believe, also true to say that, to a certain extent, there have been too many Baptisms in India instead of too few. We are learning wiser ways now ; but there was a time when it was thought right for a missionary to preach for a few days in a village, baptize any who would accept Baptism on the spot, and then leave the newly converted without any instruction or any Christian support for five or six months or longer. The result naturally was that they relapsed into practical heathenism, if indeed they had ever been really converted from it. The work of conversion, if it is to last, cannot be accomplished in that rough-and-ready fashion ; it is a plant the soil for which needs much preparation, and the after-growth long and anxious care.

Again, the difficulties connected with conversions to Christianity vary very greatly in different parts of India and among the different peoples ; the aboriginal tribes, for example, being far more open to conviction than the races which have entered India later. Again, the simple country people are easier to deal with than the educated classes, among whom at present there appear to be very special difficulties which oppose the acceptance of the Faith.

Though it may be only transitory, there does, for

example, seem in the last few years to have been a distinct attempt to revive philosophic Hinduism. That strange conglomerate known as the Chicago Parliament of Religions undoubtedly did much, if not to rekindle belief in Hinduism in the minds of the students of Calcutta, at least to feed their religious pride. The reports of the reception accorded in America to their representative, the Swami Vivekananda, was at the time in every student's mouth. Hinduism, they said, was going to convert the West, forgetful for the moment of the fact that a Hindu can only be born, he cannot become one by conversion from another faith.

When the Swami returned to Calcutta he was given a most enthusiastic reception, and became for the time a sort of Defender of the Faith. The addresses which he gave on his return served as the subject of a critical lecture which was given by Mr. Whitehead at the Mission House to a crowded audience. As a rule the Bengali student will listen with an apparent apathy which is at times one of the trials of lecturing; but on this occasion so stirred were they that something like a riot seemed for a few minutes to be imminent, and an excited demonstration in support of Vivekananda took place. Even this, hostile as it was, was preferable to the usual tone of absolute indifference to religious conviction of any kind which so largely prevails among the educated young men in Calcutta at the present time. For the revival of which we have been speaking is not a revival of *belief*, but a kind of pride in the Hindu religion as a national thing, and an organized effort to resist any weakening of its social laws.

Side by side with this exists at present another difficulty—namely, an increasing hostility to what is European and English among the educated classes. Whatever seriously affects the tone and attitude of these classes towards the English has a direct bearing on missionary work. For Christianity and the English Government are very closely bound up together in the minds of the people, even of the educated people; and therefore a growing hostility to the English means also a growing hostility to Christianity. Many of the political events of the last few years have, again, accentuated this hostile feeling. To give a single example: it is probable that the sympathy with Tilak, an editor of a Bombay paper who was recently imprisoned for sedition, is almost universal and that he is everywhere looked upon as a martyr.

A third difficulty springs from the present low standard of education. What is wanted in India, both from a political and religious point of view, is a sounder and higher education. It is not the high, but the low standard of education which is the danger. A higher education and more accurate habits of thought would soon render impossible the attempted revival of Hinduism, and compel educated men to face the questions raised by the contradictions of Hindu philosophy and the absurdities of Hindu mythology. At present an educated Hindu does not seriously consider what he believes and why he believes it. He is content with a vague adhesion to a conglomerate of contradictory beliefs; and one reason why he is content with it is because he is not trained to think deeply and probe questions to the bottom. His education trains him to move upon the surface of things; and so he does not feel the need of a thorough inquiry into first principles.

Writing in the report of the Mission in 1897, and speaking of the effect of missionary work at present among the educated classes, Mr. Whitehead wrote as follows:

"There may be, and probably is, a great deal going on beneath the surface which it is impossible for us to know; but so far as outward appearances go it cannot be said that the general body of educated Hindus are any nearer to Christianity now than they appear to have been thirty or forty years ago. Individuals, no doubt, here and there, are being drawn to CHRIST, and there is certainly 'a remnant,' both in Calcutta and elsewhere, with regard to whom there is every reason for hopefulness. But there are scarcely any signs as yet that the educated classes, as a whole, are moving in the direction of Christianity. In many respects they seem to be moving away from it. Political causes have recently produced a more decided antagonism to the English Government, and this has naturally intensified the prejudice against Christianity as the religion of the English. And at the same time the influence of Western education has been so far decidedly in the direction of indifferentism. One marked characteristic of the

University students of India, as a body, is their indifference to truth. All subjects are studied simply with the object of scoring marks at examinations, and there is absolutely none of that movement of thought and eager desire for truth that has been characteristic of Western Universities from mediæval times. This is no doubt partly due to the fact that Western modes of thought are unfamiliar to the student, and a foreign language tends to cramp his mind. But whatever the causes, the result is disastrous to the moral earnestness of the students as a class. They come to look upon truth as a thing of no intrinsic importance, and to regard contradictory systems of philosophy or religion as equally useful to the examinee. Hence there is much curiosity in Calcutta, but little desire for what is true. And in such a society we must not look for speedy results. It may be that in GOD'S providence it is necessary that this class should sink yet deeper into the slough of unbelief, and experience its bitter fruits in their moral and social life, before it is possible for them to turn to their GOD and Saviour. Meanwhile, we can only go on preaching to them the truth, and pray for their conversion, and feel thankful if we are allowed by any means to save some."

But apart from these more general influences which hinder at present the conversion of any large number of students, it has always to be remembered that every student who becomes a Christian does so at an enormous personal sacrifice and often at the risk of very real persecution. It is perhaps scarcely realized what it means to a student when he asks to be baptized, or the lengths to which at times Hindu parents will go to prevent their sons accepting Christianity. The present writer has known a case of a parent giving his son money to be used for immoral purposes in order that his sins might prevent his Baptism. Cases have been known in which parents have drugged their sons and practically made them idiots for the same purpose. It is not infrequent for a mother to threaten to take her own life if her child brings, as she considers, such disgrace upon the family as that of becoming a Christian. At the Baptism of a married man which took place at the Mission just before the present writer arrived in Calcutta, his mother-in-law did actually poison herself on the morning of his Baptism.

But short of these extreme acts, which, however, are far from uncommon, a lad who wishes to become a Christian knows that from the moment of his Baptism, as a rule, his home will be for ever closed to him ; none of his relations or friends will meet him or speak to him, or if they meet him will speak to him only to taunt him with the disgrace which he has brought upon them and upon his country. If he has any property it will be taken from him ; if he is married—and many of the students are married men—his wife and children will probably leave him. He will have to part with all that is familiar and known and dear to him, and to cast in his lot among men of another race and other modes of life and thought—perhaps among those who will rejoice over his conversion, but who will think little of showing him any warmth of brotherly love, or of giving him any real substitute for the traditions and affections of a lifetime which he has given up. If we try to think what this really means by translating it into the experience of our own life, and picturing ourselves face to face with the same consequences, we may perhaps understand what must be the moral and spiritual effort required of a Calcutta student—of one, not, like ourselves, trained to act independently and to take his own line, but accustomed from earliest infancy to think of himself only as one of a family and of a caste, and whose moral fibre, whose very sense of personality has been sapped and weakened by ages of inherited Pantheism. And yet from time to time, at the rate at present of about one or two a year, students do come forward to make a public profession of the Christian Faith.

To give a picture, which is but a sample of almost every case with which the Mission has had to deal, we will quote the account given by Mr. Strong of the Baptism of a student in 1896:

"There is some good news to tell, for another of those events has happened which are to us as flashes of lightning on a dark night—sudden gleams which illuminate our way, and show us for a moment what this land will be like when the Light has fully risen upon it. A student who had come regularly to the Hostel to read the Bible for nearly two years was convinced of the truth of Christianity; but, like so many more, had not hitherto been brave enough to profess before his relations his belief and his desire for Baptism. He felt that if he did so his mother, of whom he was very fond, would perhaps die of grief, and would certainly be almost heart-broken. But a few weeks ago he had an illness, and in the course of it he made a solemn promise to GOD that he would be prepared definitely for Baptism when he got well. For some time afterwards, however, he could not bear to face the consequences, and put it off. At last, one Sunday afternoon, when he was at the Mission House, he determined to hesitate no longer, but to stay here and write to his mother, to let her know why he had done so. He did this, and the next day his eldest brother came in great distress to say that his mother was going mad. He stayed where he was, however, and soon afterwards his mother herself came with her sons. Then ensued a scene which we shall probably never forget. His mother clung to him, howling and moaning in the strange Indian way, for more than two hours, imploring him to go back with her and not break her heart. His eldest brother also did all he could to persuade him to go. Elderly Babus from neighbouring houses shouted to him not to be so foolish and so cruel. An excited crowd collected at the gate, awaiting the issue. And there he stood—a member of a race despised by most men for its weakness —allowing his mother to cling to him, knowing that he was probably breaking her heart, feeling that his fellow-countrymen all around would despise and hate him, assured that he was giving up all

his worldly prospects, and yet able, through GOD'S
grace, to keep to his resolution! We all felt it to be
a time of intense struggle, but it ended at last. His
brother, seeing there was no hope of moving him,
took his mother away. He was baptized the next
day, and is now at Bishop's College. I have written
so much about this one event because it illustrates
so well the kind of things which have to happen
before Babus can become disciples of CHRIST. It
shows, what it is not so easy to realize in England,
what great miracles conversions are; and it may,
therefore, I think, help some of those who pray for
us and our work to offer up more of those earnest
intercessions in answer to which such miracles
happen, and without which they do not."

But the work of the Oxford Mission is not to
be gauged by the number of converts. These, as
we have tried to show, will probably at present
be very few; but that fact need not necessarily
discourage us. There is a vast amount of work
to be done which does not appear on the surface,
but which is absolutely necessary as a foundation
on which the future Church of India is to be built.
All who know India agree in thinking that when
the time is ripe the conversion of India will take
place very rapidly, and there will be sudden and
large accessions to the Church. Then it will be
shown whether the Church in India has been preparing herself for it. It is agreed on all hands
that great changes are taking place in that country.
Much that a few years ago seemed so permanent
and stable in the religious and social condition of

the people is breaking up. Western education is destroying the old beliefs; railways and other results of Western civilization are dealing hard blows at the system of caste. Ten years ago Mr. Brown, speaking at a meeting of the Oxford Mission in London, said:

"We hear a great deal about the break-up of Hinduism under the light of modern education, and it is perfectly true that there is a very great movement just now, and that we are passing through a transition time. Many of the Hindus have adopted ideas and imported infidel books from Europe, and repeat glibly the phrases found in those books; and yet I am sure that they are a race whose long tradition of centuries will never allow them to become an irreligious race. There will come, in a generation or two, a time of settling down, a time which will be a settling down of India to some form or other of religion; and I do feel it depends almost entirely upon the work which is being done now whether, when that settling down comes, they will become Christians or relapse into some form of Hinduism. When I suffer myself at all to look forward to the future with fear, the fear which most occurs to me is the danger that Hinduism, with that marvellous adaptability to circumstances which it has shown in times past, may again absorb all the elements of novelty and change which are now floating in the air, and so modify itself that people shall be able to accept it, at any rate as a social system, even in spite of the new ideas which have been flooding in upon them. And though that is

what in times of despondency I fear, it is also a
constant source of exhilaration and defence against
permanent despondency, because it makes one feel
that the work which one is doing now is foundation
work, that it must tell, if it is faithfully done, upon
the future, and that whatever is done now, however
little its results may appear upon the surface, is
needful, if the future is ever to show us the Christian Church in India."

These words are true to-day. That great and
silent revolution in thought, in faith, in custom,
which is going on so steadily in India will one day
make itself articulate; one after another the peoples
of India will have exhausted all those substitutes for
GOD wherewith men in their ignorance seek to
satisfy the needs of the human soul, and at last they
will cry for Him who alone can give them peace.
It is madness to say we will wait till the time comes,
and then make the effort to meet its demands.
When the crisis is upon us it will then be too late.
Now is the time to act; now is the time to prepare
and equip our spiritual forces; now is the time to
pour in our money, not in shillings and pence, but
in amounts proportionate to the needs, and to send
out men, not in ones and twos, but in hundreds; so
that when the day arrives there may be the Church,
ready to minister to the spiritual hunger of the vast
multitudes which will look towards her; ready with
the full teaching of the Christian Faith which alone
can satisfy the human intellect; with all the wealth
of sacramental grace which alone can supply true
moral force; with her ancient discipline, her chas-

x

tened yet splendid worship, her complete organization in the threefold ministry. Thus, and thus only, shall we be able to pay our debt to India; thus, and thus only, shall we be able to welcome into the heavenly City the peoples of that great land as they at last seek to bring their glory into it, and to become fellow-citizens with the saints and of the household of GOD.

THE RIGHT REV. HENRY WHITEHEAD, D.D.,
LORD BISHOP OF MADRAS.

[To face p. 154.

CHAPTER X

1898–1908

TEN years have been added to the history of the
Mission since this book was written, and it
devolves upon another hand than that of the author
to gather together briefly the events of this period.

The departure of Bishop Johnson was quickly
followed by another loss to the Mission scarcely less
serious. Since 1889 the Rev. Henry Whitehead had
been the Superior of the Mission, guiding its counsels
and stimulating its development with an enthusiasm
that never failed, and a power of initiative that was
ever fresh and vigorous. Early in 1898 he was
called to exercise these gifts in a wider sphere, being
appointed to the See of Madras. Though he was
thus taken away, the Mission has continued to
develop on the lines which he so wisely and firmly
laid down.

The first result of his removal was the separation
of the Mission from Bishop's College. Mr. Whitehead had held the two offices of Principal of the
College and Superior of the Mission, but there was
no necessary connection between them, and though
in this year there were some negotiations with the
S.P.G. with a view to appointing a member of the
Oxford Mission as Principal of the College, they

ultimately fell through; since then the two institutions have worked side by side, always with cordial
friendliness and mutual co-operation, but without
official connection.   Roughly speaking, the function
of the College has been to build up the life of the
Indian Christians, while the Mission has aimed more
directly at the conversion of the non-Christians;
but these are spheres of operation which cannot
be entirely separated.

The great legacy of Bishop Whitehead was the
work at Barisal, and it soon became evident that
this was capable of, and indeed called loudly for,
indefinite expansion.   Barisal is at the very centre of
the delta of the Ganges, than which there is scarcely
any more populous or fertile region in the world.
The Division[1] to which it belongs contains *eleven
million* people, considerably more than the population
of the whole of South Africa, and in this Division the

---

[1] In the Indian system of administration a Division is
that part of a Province which is under one Commissioner,
and it consists of several Districts.   The Dacca Division
contains the Districts of Dacca, Mymensingh, Faridpur, and
Barisal (sometimes called Backerganj).   Each of these Districts has a chief town of the same name.   According to the
census of 1901 the population was as follows:

Dacca District	-	2,649,522
Mymensingh District	-	3,915,068
Faridpur „	-	1,937,646
Barisal „	-	2,291,752
Total for the Dacca Division	-	10,793,988

As we must add at least 4 per cent. for the seven years
which have elapsed since the census, the population is now
well over eleven millions.   The area is 15,040 square miles,
and the number of villages and small towns rather more than
26,000.

In the Montezuma Gardens

Church of England is represented by the Oxford
Mission alone. It was obvious that the only way to
deal with such a population was to begin with the
existing Christian community; that through them,
and from them, the light must shine. For this purpose it was not enough to pay occasional visits to the
Christians in the villages, administering the sacraments, establishing schools, and giving such instruction as might be possible in the few days that such a
visit might last. Much more than this was needed,
and in the first place it was necessary that the
Mission should have a station in the heart of the
district—not two hundred miles away at Calcutta—
from which all its work should be carried on.

It was at this time, therefore, that the Brethren
began to "dream dreams" of what might be done
with the town of Barisal as a centre. Mr. Strong
and Mr. Douglass threw themselves into this scheme
with characteristic energy, and in a letter written in
1900 Mr. Strong says: "When Mr. Conway was
staying with me lately we often conjured up a vision
of what will be here one day. He was very apt at
imagining the effect upon a new-comer as the various
groups of buildings, with the church in the centre,
suddenly came in sight round certain corners; but
our vision embraced far more than the buildings.
May I give you a little sketch of what we saw?
First on the side of our land nearest to Barisal we
saw our own bungalow, with a school for Christian
boys and a training-home for teachers, catechists,
and at last, priests, on one side, and on the other a
big hostel for Hindu students. Beyond that group

we saw the church, beautiful beyond anything that
Eastern Bengal has yet imagined. Beyond that,
again, and separated from our buildings by several
large tanks and a good space of ground, we saw the
Sisters' chapel, bungalow, schools for Christian girls,
and a training-home for teachers ; and beyond that
the bungalow of the ladies who itinerate round the
district, whose big roomy boat lies at anchor in the
river, and who do such wonders in the villages and
in bringing material for the Sisters to work upon.
Then our vision passed from the buildings to those
who are to live in them. Particularly we saw the
congregation in the big church, Bengali men and
boys on one side, women and girls on the other,
Sisters dotted about amongst them. We saw reverence, order, beauty of ritual ; above all, brown faces
lit up by the light from beyond. And then we saw
many villages of the surrounding district, each a
centre of missionary activity; each with a church
built with the money and labour of the villagers—
built of bamboo and mats and thatch, or some such
common materials, but, so far as is possible to be, a
miniature of the big, beautiful church of Barisal.
We saw the congregations in these little churches
ministered to by priests of their own, who look back
to Barisal as we look back to Cuddesdon. And
lastly we saw a gathering in the Barisal church on a
festival, when the Bengali priests, catechists, and
teachers flock back to the spiritual home where they
were trained. We saw them as they gathered round
the high altar in the spacious sanctuary to sing a final
Te Deum, and as we looked into their faces we saw

[To face p. 158.

CHURCH AT BARISAL.

some—not by any means all, even yet—glowing
with holy enthusiasm for CHRIST, the apathetic
look quite gone; faces of men of whom we could
say with confidence that they were ready to leave *all*
for His sake whom they had learnt to love with a
whole-hearted devotion. And at that sight our eyes
became so full that we could see no more."

It seems marvellous that these words should have
been written only eight years ago, and already the
picture drawn by glowing faith is in a fair way of
accomplishment. The priests indeed have not come
yet—there is one supremely delicate operation of
the HOLY GHOST with which no human impatience
must be allowed to interfere—but almost everything
else in the picture is to be seen at Barisal to-day:
the church "beautiful beyond anything that Eastern
Bengal has yet imagined," the teachers, the catechists, the Sisters with their schools and training-
homes, the hostel, the village churches which are
already being built by the people with their own
labour and self-sacrifice, the reverence, the order, and
the beauty of worship. And above and beyond all
this there are the high hearts of at least a few who
are ready to leave *all* for CHRIST'S sake. One of
the latest letters says : " The Brothers have over a
hundred boys and young men in training, and are
able to have very high hopes of some of them.
Several have been working for some time past without wages to help the Mission, and now four of
them, quite of their own initiative, have resolved to
band themselves into a little Brotherhood for the
evangelization of their country. It is very interest-

ing to notice the great effect that the sight of the
Christian life, as lived by the boys, and the difference
it has made in them, makes on those who have the
opportunity of seeing it closely. I think I told you
how the Hindu contractor who built the church said
that seeing the daily life in the compound had made
him want, when he retires from business, to start a
similar school. And just lately the doctor Babu
(also a Hindu) who comes when the boys are ill has
made a considerable gift of money to help the work
by remitting a large part of his fees. They feel the
effect even if they do not understand the true cause.
And several Englishmen, too, who are not naturally
inclined to like Missions, have been very much struck
by it of late ; while one young layman in a Government office, who already cared for Church work, and
came to spend a few days with the Brothers, has
resolved to give up his post and join the Brotherhood."

There are some things almost too sacred to write
about. Let us turn to the more external aspects of
the work, which to understanding minds are true
symbols of the growth which is going on within.
And, first, of the stately church which rises like a
fairy vision in the midst of the Mission compound.
Churches in India are not often very beautiful.
They bear the impress of an economical Government which entrusts their construction to a Public
Works Department of severely utilitarian views.
From the first it was determined that the Church
of the Epiphany should be of a different character,
and a generous friend of the Mission, Mr. Thick-

MISSION SCHOOL BOYS, BARISAL.

[To face p. 160.

nesse, gave a design which in its own way can scarcely be surpassed "for glory and for beauty." The following description of it appeared in a recent number of the Oxford Mission *Quarterly Paper* :

" Our church is now all but finished, and I think the first thing which strikes every one who goes in is that they are entering a *holy* place. It is quite noticeable how this feeling makes casual English visitors silent when they go in, and the comment that the native people generally make after seeing the church is, ' I have no words.' For most of them it is the first large building they have ever been in, and the great height of the church, and its beautiful proportions, give an impression of vastness quite beyond its actual size. The church is a red-brick basilica, with an apse at the east end and a narthex containing the font at the west.

" The narthex, which is a good deal lower than the church, goes across the whole width, and gives a view into the church through three arches on slender stone pillars. This is the place where cate-chumens will be taught—they will not enter the church itself until after their Baptism. The font is octagonal and is sunk in the ground ; the Baptisms are by immersion, and are generally at Whitsuntide for converts, which is rainy weather, so we shall be glad to have the font under cover, instead of outside the old chapel as it used to be.

" A Baptism by immersion, especially of a heathen convert, is a most impressive service. A good many heathen friends and onlookers are generally present (they will be in the narthex, and the Christian con-

gregation in the church) ; the candidates wear dark
clothes ; and all the first part of the service as far as
the Baptism is at the font ; and then after a hymn,
during which the newly-baptized put on their white
clothes, the priest ' receives ' them at the entrance of
the church, and, signing them with the Cross, leads
them in, and they stand with their lighted tapers
before the altar till the service ends.

"Inside the church the south aisle is for women
and girls, and we have our Sisters' chapel at the end
of it ; at service times the boys' school and the men
are in the nave, but when the boys come into church
at other times to pray they use the north aisle.
Both the aisle-chapels are nicely private, as the
passers-by, who are allowed to come and look at
the church, only come into the narthex and see
straight up the nave and hardly at all into the aisles.
The Brothers have their chapel in the apse behind the
high altar, but we say offices together, and they come
into the sanctuary just at the side of our chapel.

"In the morning at 5.20 all the boys and girls
(except the tiny ones who are not waked for it)
come into church and sing Prime in Bengali ; it is
a simplified form with short varying lessons from
the Gospels for each day of the week. Then the
children go and we have Matins, and then the
Eucharist in English ; at a quarter to seven we go
to have some tea and fruit, and from then till Terce
at 8.30 we have a quiet time for prayer and reading
before the outside work of the day begins. These
quiet morning hours seem a sort of sanctuary where
one waits for all the strength needed for the day,

BARISAL CHURCH INTERIOR.

[To face p. 163.

and we go back there for short visits at intervals
through the day : for Sext at 12.30, None at 3,
Evensong at 6.30, and Compline at 8.30. Compline is in Bengali, and all the bigger boys and
men come ; after Compline there is silence till work
begins the next day, and we are all in bed by 9.30.
On Sundays and Saints' Days the celebration is in
Bengali, and so is Evensong the night before. I
wish you could hear the singing ; the whole congregation has a practice every day, and does it as
a work for GOD'S honour with great reverence. I
remember how much the reverence of the congregation here struck me when I first came out ; and
another noticeable thing is the absolute quiet in a
church where all the congregation are barefoot and
kneel without pews and seats.

"The church is quite undecorated at present, and
the baldacchino over the high altar is a temporary
structure of brick and wood, put up as an experiment
to see what will be the best proportions for the permanent one (one realizes out here its original use as
a protection for the altar in case of a leak from the
roof, as there has been a good deal of difficulty in
getting the roof really watertight against the tropical
storms). Some day this is to be marble, and so is
the floor of the sanctuary, while the present intention is to have the screen behind the altar and other
fittings of carved wood, inlaid with repoussé silver,
which our boys are to make. The colouring of the
church is a part of its beauty, as the bricks are very
soft in tone, and almost all the light is from the few
windows in the clerestory high above, so that it

comes down reflected and diffused instead of in a direct ray. I imagine this is partly why the interior seems to be so extremely difficult to photograph; all the attempts we have seen as yet have been complete failures.

"At present there is a thatched verandah round the church, but the design includes a cloister all round on arches, which will be a great addition to the beauty of the building—when there is money to build it. One interesting thing about the church is that the original sum of money for beginning it, R.30,000,[1] was left by a Bengali Christian lady, Mrs. Khetromoni Dutt. The building was planned by the Brothers here, who told Mr. Thicknesse (in England) exactly what they wanted; and he drew the plans and has taken infinite pains about every detail, so that we owe him a deep debt of gratitude for all the beauty of the church. It is not easy to make foundations for a large building in this part of India, where all the land is simply a deposit of Ganges mud, not many inches above the water-level; there were months of work underground before any of the walls began to rise. The first contractor was a Calcutta man; but about a year after the work was started, on one of his journeyings home, he died of plague, and then there was a long interval in the building, as his firm wanted the work, but had no one really capable of carrying it out; so it was finally entrusted to the contractor at Dacca, who

[1] About £2,000. The verandah has now been built, through the generosity of a friend, and another friend has paved the sanctuary with marble.

SOME OF THE SCHOOL BOYS AT BARISAL.

[To face p. 164.

had built the O.M. Hostel there. The local workmen had never before had to do with so large a
building, and when the walls rose high they asked
for money that they might pay one of their priests
to pray for their safety, but our Brothers explained
to them that there were two priests doing that already.
These prayers have been mercifully heard, for the
whole building has been carried through without a
single serious accident."

Mention has already been made of the Sisters, and
we must now give some account of this new and at
one time wholly unexpected development of the
Oxford Mission work.

In Calcutta the Mission is directed mainly to the
University students, who if they are married (as many
of them are) leave their wives at home when they
come up for their University course. Consequently
there had, up to the time when Barisal was taken up,
been very little demand for the services of lady
missionaries, and for what little there was, the
Brethren could always count upon the help of the
Clewer Sisters, already at work in the European
hospitals and schools, or upon their kind friends the
ladies of the Church Missionary Society and Zenana
Mission. But when Barisal was taken over with its
large Christian population, it became evident that no
real progress could be made without systematic work
amongst the women and girls ; and the conditions of
Indian life make it quite impossible that this should
be carried on by men. At first it was hoped that the
Community of S. John Baptist (Clewer Sisters)
would step into the gap, but after four or five years

of persistent application, it seemed clear that, with
the best will in the world to help, that Community
had more than enough to do to maintain its already
existing work in India.   So the Brethren resolved to
take a bold step which they have never since
regretted, namely, to start an organization of their
own, and the result is, that at the present time, there
is a fully organized Sisterhood of eleven members
under Religious vows in Barisal.   One peculiarity
about it is that it is an Indian Sisterhood; it has no
Mother-house at home, and its members are resolved
to live and die in India; they have at Shillong a
house to which they can retire for rest and change,
and though they may occasionally pay visits to
England, they are under no obligation to do so.   In
the formation of a Religious Community, more than
in most other matters, it is true that " well begun is
half done," and the Brothers were most fortunate in
being able to secure as the first head of the Community a lady who had already had great experience,
and given proof of noble qualities, as head of the
Oxford Settlement in Lambeth in connection with
Lady Margaret Hall.   Encouraged by the then
Bishop (Talbot) of Rochester, Miss Edith Langridge
resolved to obey the behest of her friend the Secretary of the Oxford Mission, and towards the end of
1902 she sailed for India with three other ladies.

It is a law of the Cross that the foundation of
great vocations must be laid deep—in great sorrows
—and during the first months of her life in India
Miss Langridge was brought almost to death's door
by severe illness; even more desolating was the trial

Sisters' House, Barisal.

[To face p. 166.

of having to part with one of the friends who had come out with her. But the end of the first year saw the little Community firmly established at Barisal, and since then it has continued to grow with the evident blessing of GOD upon it. " I look upon this as one of the most important works of my episcopate," said the Bishop of Calcutta, when he had given them their first provisional Rule, and solemnly admitted them to their probation; and now that the Rule has been carefully elaborated and tested by the experience of five years, he has given it to them again and received their first vows. All that the Brethren hoped for, and far more than they ever dared to hope for, is being accomplished by the Sisters. The Indian ladies of Barisal are visited and carefully nursed in their homes, and now that there is a lady-doctor in the Community, they will receive even more valuable help in sickness; the girls are taught in schools, and some of them are being trained to become teachers in their own villages; best of all, the unkempt, ignorant, quarrelsome women of the district, who, though Christians, had very little notion of what Christianity should mean, are being turned into reverent and sweet-tempered matrons, capable of inspiring their husbands with respect and their children with strength and purity. At a recent Confirmation the Bishop remarked upon the change which has come over the character of their worship. It is the opinion of most of those who have any acquaintance with the country that there are vast reserves of character in Indian women which will, if directed aright, lead more than anything else to the

regeneration of Indian society.   Amongst many
undesirable ideals held up by the Hindu religion, the
character of Sita in the Ramayana stands out as
pre-eminently pure, tender, and true.   It is on her
that Indian wives have chiefly tried to model themselves, not without success.   It is they who have
remained the chief support of Hinduism when it
has lost its hold upon the men of their families.   By
being withheld from education they have been prevented from taking their due share in the progress of
the Community, but still they have exercised a
marked influence from the recesses of the Zenana.
There is hardly any limit to be imagined to the
power they will exert for good, when by a Christian
education they are enabled to reach the true and
perfect development of their womanhood, and put
forth on all around them an influence no longer
marred by false and debasing ideas.   For these
reasons we may well thank GOD for the noble
beginning which has been made of an Indian Sisterhood, and look forward to the day when the
daughters of India themselves shall be gathered
into it, to learn there those lessons of spiritual
discipline and burning love which shall make them
the servants of their race for high and glorious ends.

   The town of Barisal is sixteen miles from the
nearest, and about fifty miles from the farthest
of the villages, and in order to be still nearer their
people Mr. Conway and Mr. Cooke have recently
made a new settlement at a place called Jobarpar in
the very centre of their district; and here, too, a
couple of the Sisters generally reside.   The expense

NATIVE HUTS AT JOBARPAR. MEN MAKING A HUT WALL.

[To face p. 168.

of starting this new establishment was generously borne by the father of one of the missionaries.

This picture of life at Barisal seems almost ideal. There has, however, been one most serious drawback. The political agitations of the last few years have produced a state of tension which has been most inimical to direct missionary work. All Englishmen are put in the same category, and the sins, or supposed sins, of the Government are visited on the missionaries. Consequently the Brethren have found it impossible to get into any sort of touch with the non-Christians around them ; the small hostel which was at one time started has been empty ; and, worst of all, a convert was spirited away after his Baptism, and has, it is feared, gone back to Hinduism. Thus, while the Christian life at Barisal has been developing with every sign of abundant blessing, the impression made upon the Hindus and Mussulmans around has apparently been none at all. We say "apparently," for it is often during such times of discouragement that the way is being secretly prepared for a great advance, and already there are signs that the bitterness of the opposition is passing away, and Hindu students are beginning to return to the hostel. Moreover, the work of the Sisters has been quietly effective for the wide promotion of good will.

It must not be forgotten that the original *raison d'être* of the Oxford Mission, never lost sight of, was the work amongst the University students. If there is any one class which will be influential in making or marring the future of the country it is the Bengali students. It is they from whom springs the whole

z

tribe of political agitators, and amongst whom the
agitators find their most ardent pupils; it is they
who have formed the backbone of the National
Congress; and in every walk of life where mind
rather than muscle is required it is the Bengali who
pushes to the front. There is a good side to all this.
The energy which expends itself in political vapour-
ing can be directed into useful channels, and all over
India Bengali Babus are to be found in positions of
influence. The Cambridge Mission at Delhi have
made a noble venture by appointing a Bengali to
succeed an Englishman in the headship of their
College, and this is only a conspicuous instance of
what is happening in many other places. Thus it is
evident that to capture the Bengali student for
CHRIST would be to make an important step
towards the evangelization of India; and though
the work has proved slow and difficult, we may well
feel that it is hard because it is high. The few
converts from this class made by the Oxford
Mission have been of the very best, and it would
be difficult to overrate their influence for good.
One of them, who is now at Barisal, is a man whom
one cannot know without being impelled both to
admiration and to love, and his work in the Mission is
one of daily increasing power and spirituality. Thus,
while the work amongst uneducated villagers has all
the charm and privilege of preaching the Gospel to
the poor, we may not forget that we are debtors
" both to the Greeks and to the barbarians, both to
the wise and to the unwise." Consequently, the
Mission was ready to welcome an opportunity of

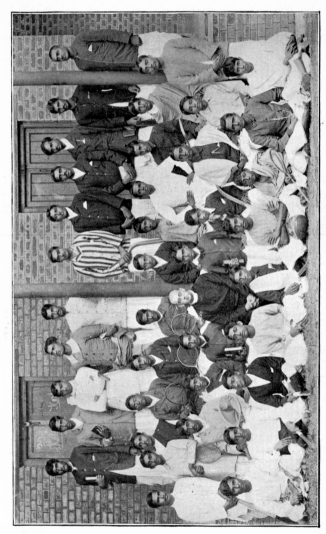

OXFORD MISSION HOSTEL, DACCA, 1908-1909.

extending its work in this direction, which came during the short episcopate of Bishop Welldon.

Next to Calcutta, Dacca is the most important town of Lower Bengal. It has a population of nearly 100,000; it was at one time the capital of the Mussulman rulers; and it occupied a position which, since the creation of Eastern Bengal into a separate Province, has led to its becoming the capital. The Baptists have done excellent work there, and the Roman Catholics have a strong Mission in one part of the district, but not very much attention had been paid to the student class, and they had the reputation of being even more unruly, less amenable to discipline, than their compatriots in other places. It was in 1900 that Bishop Welldon paid a visit to the place, and delivered a lecture to the students which was listened to with much attention. He came back with a heart filled with yearning over these sheep without a shepherd, and at once approached the Oxford Mission with a view to some permanent work being established there. It was a field towards which the Brethren had often cast longing eyes, and though the call came at a time when the staff was more than usually depleted, they felt it was one not to be resisted. All that could be done at first was to arrange for a fortnightly visit, but from that beginning has gradually grown up, under the able supervision of Mr. Teignmouth Shore, a regular Mission station with a hostel for forty students.

The opening of the Dacca Hostel, on January 24, 1905, was a great day in the history of the Mission.

Bishop Mylne, in his *Missions to Hindus*, after discussing various methods of missionary work, writes:
" The Oxford Mission at Calcutta seems to me to
have solved the problem more nearly than any other
society. It has no college of its own. It is not an
educational Mission. But its missionaries devote
much time to the welfare of native students by
helping them morally and spiritually, and even by
assisting them in their studies. Under the Indian
University system hundreds of Hindu youths, from
every part of the country, are thrown into the bazaars
unprotected, and are left to shift for themselves, as
regards all care for their characters, till the *disrepute*
of a neighbourhood is what renders it attractive as a
lodging-place. To boys thus utterly uncared for the
Mission opens its doors. It has established a hostel
for them, where they may live the lives of Hindus,
only having opportunities afforded them of forming
acquaintance with the missionaries, and of learning
from intimacy with them what the Christian religion
means."

There has been no reason to feel dissatisfied with
the method thus commended by one of the greatest
living authorities on the subject, and to extend it to
Dacca was a natural corollary of the success it has
met with in Calcutta. The Dacca Hostel has been
full from the moment it was built. After a recent
visit the Director of Public Instruction for Eastern
Bengal wrote to Mr. Teignmouth Shore: " I can
only say I was immensely impressed with the work
you and Mr. Manley are doing."

In Calcutta, too, the hostel has had an encourag-

DACCA HOSTEL.

[*To face p. 172.*]

ing history. From its small beginning in a hired
house it has now flourished into a stately mansion
adjoining the Mission House, with room for more
than forty students. Latterly it has been under the
management of Mr. Holmes, who joined the Mission
in 1903, after being for seven years Vicar of S. Peter's,
Jarrow. His watchful care and genial wisdom have
guided it through troublous times. During all the
political agitation and anti-English feeling of the last
few years it has never failed to be well filled ; indeed
the number of applications for admission has been
as much as ten times in excess of the accommodation. That the work which these hostels are doing
is appreciated by the Government is shown by the
generous grants—Rs.20,000 for Dacca, and Rs.25,000
for Calcutta—which were made to the respective
building funds. The ground of these grants is no
doubt that the work done by hostels is of social
benefit to the Community, but of course the Brethren
value them also, and chiefly, for the great missionary
opportunity which they afford. A former inmate of
the Calcutta Hostel, writes : " Excuse me if I tell
you what I sincerely feel. Our hostel is the only
place in Calcutta where young college students
breathe a pure moral atmosphere. Boys may go
away from the hostel without being converted to
Christianity, but they surely carry with them some
influence for good, at least they cease to look upon
us Christians as great scoundrels." Not the least of
the advantages of the hostel is that the example set
by the Oxford Mission in starting it has been
followed by several other Missionary Societies.

To complete the picture of this side of the work, let us turn once more to the little Mission paper, the *Epiphany*, which has now been published weekly for more than twenty-five years. In the Report for 1907 Mr. Holmes writes: "The *Epiphany* continues to do its good work. We have never been more hopeful as to its influence than we are now. Its circulation is well over 10,000 weekly, and we frequently receive evidence from different parts of India that it is helping people. For instance, last week a postmaster in the South of India wrote to say that he could not sufficiently express his gratitude to the *Epiphany*, as through it he and his family had been led to Baptism. Another letter, also from the South of India, was received earlier in the year saying that the paper had roused the educated Hindus in the neighbourhood to violent opposition, with the result that the demand for the *Epiphany* was largely on the increase, and to meet the cost of the increased circulation the magistrate of the district had given a considerable donation. Two colleges in Delhi and Allahabad have asked that a series of articles, which have appeared this year, may be published in book form. Many similar testimonies could be given." The Bishop of Birmingham said in a speech that he considered the *Epiphany* "one of the most wonderful papers on the face of the globe. . . . You cannot conceive in England the gulf which yawns between the life of the Englishman and the life of the native, though the English and the natives are touching one another physically every day. . . . This *Epiphany* with its medium of com-

GROUP OF MEMBERS OF THE MISSION, 1904.

[To face p. 174.

munication, with its correspondence column, acts as a link between the thought of the Englishman and the thought of the Indian. It is quite invaluable; there is really nothing like it in India, and the real work which the *Epiphany* has done in bringing round English thought into communication with the thought of the people in the country is extraordinary." Besides what is published in the paper the editor is often brought into very sacred and intimate communication with correspondents whom he answers privately. Perhaps one such letter may be admitted here, because it is exactly typical of the state in which we believe thousands to be existing in the present day in India. The writer began by sending a letter to the *Epiphany* in which he urged one of the correspondents of the paper to embrace Christianity. The editor wrote to him privately, pointing out the inconsistency of advising others to become Christians while he was himself a Hindu. The following was his reply :—

" DEAR SIR,

" This letter from me may perhaps take you by surprise, as I am myself to be introduced to you first of all. Some months back I sent you a letter as a reply to Mr. Rama Krishna's question, urging him to become a Christian, and signed 'M. Govindam,' for publication in your *Epiphany*. Before its publication you sent me a letter advising me first of all to become a Christian. I know well I have not well behaved in not writing you a reply. But, Sir, there were reasons for it. I was in a dilemma, and I did

not know what to write to you.   From what follows
you could almost realize my situation.

" My life, so far as religion is concerned, is a
curious if not a miserable one.   For a few years, in
the beginning of my scholastic career, when I was
but a boy of nine or ten, I was a thorough Christian
at heart; but when I grew up, and when I began to
know the world, and when tit-bits of science began
to enter my head, my faith began to waver, and
ultimately wore away, and I became one of those
who look down with contempt upon Faith and its
dogmas, and who disdain to believe in anything but
what is established by Reason and Science.   But
again the scene changed, and when the Bible began
to be studied daily in the class the old *Belief*, but
not Faith, began to return.   With the most impressive and kindly advice of the missionary manager of
our school (I passed my Matric. only last year) the
Belief increased, and a fight between *Belief* and
Doubt began to ensue and distress my soul.   After
I came out of the school I confined myself to the
study of the New Testament alone.   This has been
the most critical stage of my religious life.   I could
write out my thoughts now in volumes, but sorry for
want of space here.   To be brief, in the incessant
struggle between *Doubt* and *Faith*, the latter
ultimately almost gained.   Sometimes while reading the Bible I felt myself a very, very happy one,
and praised GOD and CHRIST.   But at times there
was also the strong adversary Doubt prevailing, and
then my heart became sad and cold, lost all its
enthusiasm, and I felt I was a very miserable crea-

ture. But constant reading of the Bible got rid of
this, and Faith reasserted itself, and it was at this
time, when I happened to see Mr. Rama Krishna's
question, that I wrote him a reply in the joy of my
heart.   But adverse circumstances prevented me
from reading the Bible often, though not entirely.
But again it is some time that I have begun to read
the Bible diligently, and again the most heartrending
fight has begun.   And indeed it must be so in such
a place as this, where criticisms against Christianity
by learned Hindus, etc., are never wanting.   Sometimes, when with full faith I go out, I meet with
persons who tell me, 'Why do you believe in
Christianity, which contains absurd theories of
Creation which are refuted by all scientific men?
Even many Europeans of high culture believe in
Transmigration. JESUS CHRIST was taken only
half-conscious from the Cross, but not dead,' etc.

"The manager of our school, a German missionary,
an extremely good and kind and pious gentleman,
used to advise me that an electric power exists in
Baptism, telling me the illustration that the action in
an electric battery begins when and only when the
pole wires are joined together; and I too, from my
childhood up to this, have wished to become a
Christian inwardly as well as outwardly.   But, Sir,
what is my state? Circumstances can never be so
strong against any one else.   To realize it one must
be in my state.   Leaving aside all other considerations, let me say that to become a Christian means
to forsake all my relations and friends, and my sweet
mother and sisters.   That seems an impossibility to

me, and when I think so I feel extremely sorry. Truly I remember CHRIST'S saying, ' He who loves father, etc., more than Me is not worthy of Me.' But hard circumstances! Many a time have I thought within myself, ' What! I will go and receive Baptism just now.' But the next moment I lose the courage, and the thought vanishes away. Every day I use to read my Bible and offer my prayer through CHRIST, even to-day.

" Truly when I see my Christian friends I envy their lot that made them Christians by birth. It is because I am born a Hindu that I have this great ordeal before me. I have the greatest wish to embrace Christianity, but I sadly know I never can. I have written this letter not because I know you will show me a new way of overcoming these difficulties, but that you may heartily pity my state and pray to GOD to give me *new* strength and courage to sacrifice myself for Him."

In a letter written more than a year later the writer announces that he has at last found courage to be baptized. Would that all such conflicts might end so happily!

There is little to add to what has been said above about the school in Calcutta. It continues to do a useful work, and, in conjunction with the similar school for girls carried on by the Clewer Sisters, is helping to change the face of the Christian community and to build it up on that soundest of all foundations—a true and reverent family life. One of the old boys of the Oxford Mission School has found his way to England, and is there carrying on a good work among the lascars at Birkenhead in connection with the Mersey Mission to Seamen. Another has a Government appointment as doctor to a West African force, and when one remembers that Bengalis have been called a race that never held a sword, it is rather fine to hear that he has gone on a military expedition, and even at one time, in the absence of other officers, was in command of it. The experience of these boys is a good illustration of the way in which Christianity sets the Hindu free to develop all his powers for the common good, and rise to the height of his manhood. As one of themselves wrote: "There is still a dead weight of caste prejudice and superstition lying like a curse on the country. It is only the Indian Christian who finds himself really free, and, therefore, able to devote himself to new pursuits. The dissatisfaction with the old standard of life and thought finds its culminating point in him. Education added to his religious and social freedom brings high professional prizes within his grasp. His origin may be low, his income small, but he is free in the real sense of the word. He has secured the freedom required to live up to the new and enlightened standard of life. There are no caste-fellows to cramp his ambition. There is no uneducated wife or mother to thwart him at every hour. He has no child-wife growing up with him to nip his youth and manhood in the bud. He has broken with a dozen stale, obsolete customs, which cramp and limit the energies of his heathen countrymen. A Hindu or a Mohammedan with English education may consider himself a child of freedom ;

but his freedom is prison life compared with the freedom of an Indian Christian."

Even those who would not support Missions on what we should hold to be the truest and deepest grounds may well consider whether in these words we have not an indication that without Christianity India can never rise to its true stature, intellectual, spiritual, and moral.   For, indeed, the old order in India is changing, and that which is taking its place is in reality founded on the Christian ideal, though that ideal is as yet very imperfectly realized.   A few years ago the aspect of the country could well be described as one of stagnation.   There was no clear indication that it would ever wake up from its old lethargy. Lord Acton has described Hinduism as a stationary religion, and those who know it best, in its effects, would go further and say that it is not only stationary but retrogressive ; by the testimony of the Hindus themselves, its Golden Age is not in the future but in the past.   Matthew Arnold has summed up its spirit with marvellous insight in the well-known verse—

> " The East bow'd low before the blast
>   In patient, deep disdain ;
> She let the legions thunder past,
>   And plunged in thought again."

And that thought was for ever turned in upon itself, unfruitful, unpractical, unprogressive.   The really great intellectual achievements of India in the past have in the modern world sunk to a mere repetition of barren formulas.   But during the last fifty years a great revolution has been silently preparing, and the

SHILLONG—CHAPEL AND SISTERS' REST HOUSE BEYOND.

[To face p. 181.

revolution is the result of that Western education which substitutes Christian for Hindu ideals. It would be a great mistake to look upon this revolution as wholly evil because it has some unpleasant manifestations on the surface ; but whether evil or not, it was wholly inevitable, and our business is to meet it, not in a spirit of reactionary panic, but with sympathy and hopefulness. We must try to offer our continued guidance to the people of India in such a way as to show them the true goal of all their efforts. Thus, we feel sure that there is a great future before the Oxford Mission, and all similar Missions to the educated classes in India, not in the way of an immediate accession of converts, but in the good which must come from the patient and persevering exhibition of a true ideal. Hinduism has never made a great nation, and never will. Its influence is disintegrating, through the caste system ; debilitating, through the moral indifference engendered by a Pantheistic creed ; degrading, through the base examples of its deities. The utter poverty of its ideals is exemplified by the fact that the national party has been compelled to make a hero of such a character as Sivaji. Christianity and Mohammedanism alone among religions have been the nursing mothers of great nations; but Mohammedanism has had its chance in India, and though there are now some sixty million Mohammedans in the country, they are not the men to whom India looks for light or leading. In spite of themselves patriotic Indians are turning more and more towards Christianity as that which can alone give them hope and inspiration. The speeches at the National Congress, and on other occasions, are constantly filled with quotations from the Bible; the regulations of the National Service League read like the Rule of one of our Religious Orders. It will depend entirely on the way in which the Church fulfils her duty during the present century, on the power and purity with which she bears her witness to the one Ideal of all humanity, whether or not India will at last open her eyes to see that in this alone lies her hope of becoming—what she is now striving to be—a nation really great, capable of taking its due place among the kingdoms of the earth, and of becoming a fruitful training-ground for the ripening of souls for eternity.

SNAKE CHARMER AND COBRA.

[*To face p.* 183.

CHAPTER XI

HINDUISM AS IT IS [1]

" Dark is the world to thee; thyself art the reason why,
   For is He not all but thou, that hast power to feel 'I
      am I'?
   Glory about thee, without thee: and thou fulfillest thy
      doom,
   Making Him broken gleams, and a stifled splendour and
      gloom."

ANY history of the Oxford Mission to Calcutta
would be incomplete without some account,
however inadequate, of the present state of Hindu
religious thought as it is met with among the
educated classes. The present writer cannot do
more than put together very briefly an outline of
some aspects of modern Hinduism as they presented
themselves to him while he was in Calcutta. But
he does so in the hope that it may help the readers
of this history to realize the difficulty of the work
among the educated Hindus, and so allay that
impatience with which the progress of Indian Missions is so often judged, as well as to dissipate the
illusions of those who may have accepted the somewhat common idea that Hinduism is a religion which,

---

[1] In the following chapter free use has been made of
articles which have been published in the *Epiphany* and in the
Oxford Mission *Quarterly Papers*.

though inferior to Christianity, possesses a fairly practical moral power. For a really luminous and masterly account of modern Hinduism the writer wishes to refer to the first and second series of Sir Alfred Lyall's *Asiatic Studies*, and more especially to the admirable discussion of the subject in the first chapter of the second series.

I. THE EXTREME VAGUENESS OF HINDUISM

The first point on which we wish to dwell is the extreme vagueness of Hinduism. Whatever differences there may be on many questions among Christians, they can all accept the Apostles' Creed as the formula of their faith. In that concise and nervous statement is found the outline of the Christian belief. But no such formulary of belief exists among Hindus; at least, repeated challenges to Hindu gentlemen to produce any such formula have always failed to elicit any reply. But a statement as to what Hinduism is was evoked from a leading native paper in Calcutta in the early part of 1894. It was published under the following circumstances. In April of that year the *Banga Bashi*, a native newspaper, in giving the account of the suicide of a child-widow aged eleven, concluded with the words, "*It is her fate.*" The *Epiphany*, in commenting on these words, asked to be enlightened as to the meaning attached to the word "fate" by orthodox Hindus. It was in answer to this question that the paragraph which follows was published in the *Indian Nation*. This is the ablest and best-conducted of the native papers in Calcutta, and its editor is a

gentleman who has been in England and has had
the advantages of both an Eastern and Western
education. He is himself a Hindu, and therefore
speaks from within Hindu society and religious
thought. This is his account of Hinduism as it
now is :—

"We shall not undertake to answer the last
question in any direct or definite form.[1] But from
all the expositions of Hinduism that we have
recently been reading we should be justified in
saying that Hinduism does not believe in a
FATHER, does not believe in a personal GOD at
all, does not believe in any god who is not the sub-
stance of a universe coeval with himself, does not
therefore believe in responsibility to a supreme
Being, does not believe in any conscious award of
reward and punishment. All that happens to a
man in this world is only the consequence necessarily arising from his actions in a previous life in
this world; his actions in this present life will
determine his lot in his next birth, and so on, until
by sinlessness he becomes absorbed in the divine
essence and so saved from future births. What sin
or sinlessness can mean in such a system we shall
not take upon ourselves to answer. Man's life is
a chain of necessities; divine operations are necessities also. GOD does not will to create; the universe,
always existent in Him, is unfolded by a necessity.
Not being a person, He lays down no moral law
which it would be a sin to disobey. Obedience and

---

[1] i.e., the meaning attached by orthodox Hindus to the
word " fate."

disobedience have, in fact, no meaning, as man is
not a free agent. That seems to be the interpretation of Hinduism now prevalent in Bengal. How
far it is correct we shall not seek to discuss. Those
who offer the interpretation are so confident in its
correctness that they would treat as idiots all who
differed from them. A correspondent who often
addresses us on Hinduism in an authoritative way
informed us the other day that creation, a personal
GOD, and free-will were indefensible doctrines and
impossible conceptions."[1]

Surely the words we have just quoted throw a
significant light on the condition of modern Hinduism, and the more significant in that, as we have
said, it comes from one not without, but within,
the Hindu religion. We say " religion," but the
word is a misnomer, for what place can there be
for religion, in any real sense of the word, if the
GOD towards whom man's religion is directed is not
a personal Being ?

This utterance of the *Indian Nation* was succeeded
in the following May by an article in the same
journal entitled " Protean Hinduism," in which the
writer shows how various are the forms in which
Hinduism is held by different teachers. And herein
lies one of the chief difficulties which a missionary
experiences in dealing with it. What is it he
has to attack ? Where is he to begin ? How is
he to deal with a religion which one of its own
supporters thus describes as being mostly a series
of negations ?

[1] The *Indian Nation*, April 30, 1894.

But this is not all. Hinduism, as it meets us to-day among the educated classes in Calcutta, not only baffles attack from its extreme vagueness, and the rapidity and ease with which it is ever adapting itself to new forms, and discovering new authorities in its sacred books to sanction the ever-increasing demands of Western civilization and Western education, but it has an added difficulty in its apparent capacity for holding what to a Western mind appear to be bewildering contradictions.

A few weeks after the issue of the extract from the *Indian Nation* to which we have just referred, the editor of the same paper had occasion to criticize a speech made by the Lieutenant-Governor of Bengal at a missionary meeting at Darjeeling, in which criticism were the following words :—

"Hinduism is more an affair of life than of doctrine. The Hindu will not ordinarily be convinced of the superiority of a religion which permits the slaughter of kine for food and of men for conquest. He believes in a religion which inculcates physical purity and asceticism, which makes a sin of killing, and which permits of no flagging of spiritual interests. A religion which extends its sanction to war, butchery, and diplomacy will not appear to him spiritual enough ; and games, sports, dancing, and such other Western accomplishments will strike him as unpardonable levity in a minister of religion. His admiration is reserved for the *Yogi* ; and he has no appreciation of the clergyman who wins a bride by courtship and dines and drives in state. He is an hourly witness of miracles, and will not limit his

faith to those few recorded in one sacred book. He
believes in the capacity of prayer to bring down the
divine influence to human souls and even to clay
images. Religion is to him, if it is to anybody,
other-worldliness—absolute, absorbing, all-compre-
hending—and not a mere regulation of *this*-worldli-
ness. Let the missionary therefore well understand
his customer before he sets about his business. If
he is prepared with a more spiritual and less worldly
ideal than the Hindu, he may do something. But
he certainly will not do anything if, instead of
forgetting distinctions of colour, he emphasizes them
and gives to the 'heathen,' newly admitted into
light, another caste in place of the one he was made
to renounce." [1]

We think that any one who reads this and the
former extract together will not think we have
been unjust in speaking of the capacity of the Hindu
mind for holding statements which are mutually contradictory. And to substantiate our charge still
further we will quote a criticism made in the
Epiphany on these same two passages :—

" If inability to grasp the primary law of thought,
that a thing cannot at the same time be and not be,
exhibits a convincing proof of 'spirituality,' then
certainly the ideal Hindu, as depicted by the *Indian
Nation*, may lay claim to the possession of that
quality in a very high degree. According to our
contemporary, the primary article of the Hindu's
'creed' (if we may be allowed the expression) is
that ' GOD, not being a person, lays down no moral

[1] The *Indian Nation*, June 11, 1894.

law which it would be a sin to disobey,' and he proceeds to act upon this belief by ' making a sin of killing even kine for food or of men for conquest '; while his chief ceremonial expression of it is prayer, which ' brings down the divine influence to human souls and even to clay images ! ' If the ' spiritual ' is really equivalent to the irrational, we must wish GOD-speed to materialism.

"Other contradictions are involved, which are not expressed. The true Hindu, we are told, believes in the sinfulness of ' war, butchery, and diplomacy ', and a religion which extends its sanction to these is intolerable to him. But the most sacred hymns of his religion consist largely of prayers for victory over enemies in battle, while its epics deal, like all epics, with war and bloodshed, in which the gods themselves take part. Nay, more, he believes the warrior caste to have had a divine origin second only to the priestly. As to diplomacy, we can only wish that we met more Hindus who disapproved of it.

"Again, we are told that ' games, sports, dancing, and such other Western accomplishments strike him as unpardonable levity in a minister of religion.' In this we may agree with him ; but it seems slightly odd, to say the least of it, that the most popular of all the deities should be celebrated for precisely such accomplishments as well as others less innocent ; and we can only wish the Brahman caste—the chief ' ministers of religion '—indulged in no worse diversions.

"Again, if ' spirituality ' and ' other-worldliness '

are chiefly betokened by the asceticism which
delights in finding impurities in the use of material
things, and in legislating for these with greater
emphasis and elaboration than for grave moral
trespasses, we may concede that the Hindu out-
shines all others in the possession of these virtues—
even the Pharisees, whose bondage to physical and
ceremonial ideas of impurity brought them into such
violent collision with the teaching of CHRIST.
'Other-worldliness' we should take to mean such
an absorption in spiritual things as lifts a man's
mind above these trivial distinctions, rather than the
spirit which exhibits itself in their multiplication—
'touch not, taste not, handle not'—a legalism which
could not be better described than as 'a system of
regulated this-worldliness,' and an aggravated type
of it. The teachings of CHRIST and of S. Paul are
certainly most 'worldly' and 'unspiritual' from this
point of view."

In July of the same year the editor of the
Epiphany was again in controversy with the *Indian
Nation* on the question of the contradictoriness of
its statements as to the belief of Pantheists in a
personal GOD. The *Indian Nation*, in an indignant
article, accused the *Epiphany* of misrepresenting its
meaning, and it was in vindication of his assertion
that the editor printed the following extracts from
the *Indian Nation* in parallel columns :—

"Pantheism is objected to
by our contemporary for the
reason that Pantheists elimi-
nate from the conception of
what they call the 'divine'

"He must have heard of
the Pantheists. Do they
believe in a personal GOD ?
And yet have they not felt
it permissible to speak of a

the idea of personality. We are afraid the *Epiphany* has again missed the mark of distinction between Theism and Pantheism. Pantheism, as far as we understand it, by no means eliminates or discards the idea of a personal GOD, but the idea of a *separate* personal GOD. To the Pantheist GOD is personified by the universe at large. The Theist may think otherwise : to him GOD may be a personality distinct from the universe; but whether distinct from or personified by the universe, there is the conception of a divine personality in both systems."— *Indian Nation*, November 13, 1893.

moral GOD and a divine influence ? " — *Indian Nation*, July 2, 1894.

"Our contemporary asserts that some time last year we maintained vigorously the position that Pantheists do believe in a personal GOD. It is the simple truth that we never maintained any such position, either last year or at any other period of our existence, vigorously or otherwise. . . . *We* never declared that Pantheists do believe in a personal GOD. . . . The *Epiphany*, of all papers, should have been the last to fight a battle with weapons no better than limping logic and perversions of fact." — *Indian Nation*, July 9, 1894.

It would be difficult, one would have thought, even for the 'ideal Hindu,' to blink the contradictions here exhibited ; but all that it evoked from the *Indian Nation* was an angry and scornful article on the gross dullness of the Western intellect.

II. HINDUISM A SOCIAL SYSTEM

Let us turn now to another exponent of modern Hinduism, Mr. Guru Prasad Sen. According to Mr. G. P. Sen, Hinduism is not a religion, but a social system. We are bound to confess that to one living in Calcutta the social side of Hinduism is much more prominent than the religious side. It is not, for example, the breach of the moral law, but the transgression of caste rules, which really touches

what, for want of another word, we must call the
conscience of a Hindu. To tell a lie is nothing;
to eat with a foreigner, or with a Hindu of a lower
caste, is a heavy sin, for which a definite and
elaborate purification must be undergone.   Again,
while the mass of students would not, openly at any
rate, contravene the laws of their caste, prayer is
practically unknown among them.   But let us listen
to Mr. Guru Prasad Sen as he explains Hinduism
to us in " An Introduction to the Study of Hinduism" which appeared as an article in the *Calcutta
Review* :—

"Hinduism is not, and never has been, a religious
organization. It is a purely social system, which
insists for those who are Hindus on the observance
of certain social forms, and not on the profession
of any particular religious beliefs.   It has not
even a religious creed or a common set of beliefs,
nor has it for its guide a particular book, though
popularly the Vedas and Shastras are credited with
being the books of the Hindus. So far as religious
beliefs are concerned, Hinduism embraces within
its fold all phases of belief and even of unbelief,
from the extreme agnosticism of the Nastics and
Charbaks to the popular polytheistic creed of the
believers in the myriads of Hindu gods and god-
desses. The Hindu Shastras are, to use a Hindu
metaphor, a vast ocean, which, so far as religion is
concerned, the votary, like the Hindu gods of old,
has only to churn to find the nectar of truth which
is exactly suited to the light that is in him.   It is
perfectly optional with a Hindu to choose from any

one of the different religious creeds with which the Shastras abound ; he may choose to have a faith and creed, if he wants a creed, or to do without one. He may be an atheist, a deist, a monotheist, or a polytheist, a believer in the Vedas or Shastras, or a sceptic as regards their authority; and his position as a Hindu cannot be questioned by anybody because of his beliefs or unbeliefs so long as he conforms to social rules."

III. HINDUISM AND SIN

Once again let us question Hinduism as to its teaching on the all-important and universal fact of sin. In answer we will quote from a speech made at the Chicago Parliament of Religions by Babu N. N. Dutt, known as the Swami Vivekananda, who was the representative of the Hindu religion at that extraordinary assemblage. In the course of his speech he made use of the following words :—

"Allow me to call you, brethren, by that sweet name *heirs of immortal bliss*: yea, the Hindus refuse to call you sinners. Ye are the children of GOD, the sharers of immortal bliss. Ye, divinities on earth, sinners ? It is a sin to call man so. It is a standing libel on human nature. Come up, O lions, and shake off the delusion that you are sheep : you are souls immortal, spirits free and blest and eternal. Ye are not matter, ye are not bodies. Matter is your servant, not you the servants of matter."

"According to Hindu philosophy, sin is a complete delusion : there is really no such thing at all, thus justifying Babu N. N. Dutt's statement.

Individual existence being an illusion — a sort of mysterious disease that has crept over the one universal existence—it follows that the offences and faults for which the illusory individual conscience blames itself are equally unreal. The supreme essence is of course in itself sinless, only somehow it dreams itself into individuality and sinfulness. The real object of life in Hinduism is not a moral one at all, but a purely intellectual one—i.e., not to get rid of sin, but to rid ourselves of the idea that we are sinners.

"And yet, this being its philosophy, what do we behold in practice? There are few beliefs so vitally held as that of *Karma*, which teaches that sins bring terrible punishments—that as men sow, so must they reap, in this life and in future lives. The laws of Manu and Vishnu contain elaborately detailed lists of the fearful penalties attaching in the next world to the chief sins against Hindu morality, along with equally elaborate prescriptions of the various expiations, penances, tortures, self-macerations—sometimes approaching suicide—by which alone these sins can be atoned for in the present life. The Hindu apparently acts upon the belief of the reality of sin, accepts the verdict of his conscience, while yet he holds both sin and conscience to be of the nature of illusion. How the theory and practice are reconcilable is more than any Hindu has ever yet succeeded in explaining, the only explanation being that 'Hinduism' is a mass of incoherent, inconsistent, hopelessly irreconcilable beliefs, jumbled together under a common name—Theism, Panthe-

ism, Polytheism, Atheism, all alike sheltering themselves under it." [1]

The members of the Brahmo Somaj have indeed
a more definite and clear conception of sin than the
orthodox Hindu, but they themselves acknowledge
that they have derived their sense of sin from Christian teaching. They certainly could not have got
it from Hinduism, for according to Hinduism, as
expounded at least by Babu N. N. Dutt, the soul is
already perfectly blest, but it fails to recognize that
it is so.

Let us listen, again, to another Hindu, Babu
Gurudip Sing. In a letter written by him in the
Epiphany of July 5, 1895, on the " Ideals of Hinduism," he makes the following statements with regard
to the Hindu view of sin—statements which he
quotes with approval as expressing the mind of an
orthodox Hindu :—

" Sankaracharya [2] plainly says that the ideas,
namely (1) that I am a sinful man, (2) that there
must be some supreme Being having power to free
me from my sins and to give me eternal heavenly
life, etc., etc., are emanations of an imperfect mind.
He who has obtained the light of true knowledge
will never entertain such ideas. . . . From what you
(i.e., the *Epiphany*) write, it seems that you think it
impossible to get rid of sin by the knowledge of
Brahma. [3] No : we do get rid of sin by its know-

---

[1] *Epiphany*, May 31, 1895.

[2] A great religious teacher and reviver of Brahmanism.
He lived about the end of the seventh or the beginning of
the eighth century.

[3] The supreme Being.

ledge. You know that ideas create ideas, and at the
same time they destroy each other. For example,
the idea of some serious illness results in the idea of
death, which again in its turn gives rise to the idea of
sorrow, and so on. But the idea of some successful
remedy or medicine at the same time counteracts the
idea of serious illness, and thus the man who should
have otherwise experienced sorrow now enjoys peace
of mind. In the same way, the idea of Brahma
destroys the idea of sin altogether. The Hindu
idea of sinfulness is just the same as the Christian
idea [!]; *and we want to get rid of the idea of not sin
only, but virtue also,* because you know they are
co-relatives, and the retention of either of them is
equally fatal to the uniform and undisturbed peace
of mind. . . ."

The italics in the above paragraph are our own.
The sentence illustrates a very prevalent idea in
Hindu thought—namely that vice and virtue are
both equally illusions, and that the aim of the perfect
Hindu is to rise superior to both, to reach a state
in which he becomes alike indifferent to virtue as
well as to vice. To show that we are not misrepresenting Hinduism on this point, we will quote
the answer given to the following question, to which
the *Epiphany* asked for a reply from an orthodox
Hindu. The question was as follows:—

" Is it the ideal of Hinduism to realize sinfulness
and to obey the voice of conscience, or to get rid of
both ? "

To this the following reply was received.

" The Hindu considers it his duty to realize sin-

fulness and to obey the voice of conscience *so long as
he has not practically realized that he is the absolute*,
or in other words, as long as he has not mingled
his consciousness with the spirit of nature. The
Yogi [1] has no attraction or repulsion either for
heaven or hell. The state of the *Yogi* is above
that in which there is longing for any object. *The
wise never praises the good, nor does he hate the bad.
Equal in happiness and misery, he thinks himself
above duty.*"

The italics are again our own; and the whole
answer illustrates what has to be constantly borne
in mind in studying Hinduism—that the great object
of life is an intellectual, not a moral one: virtue and
vice and conscience are all "illusion," and the con-
templation of the indifference of good and evil is
one of the means by which that object is to be
reached. The description of "the wise man" as
given in the above answer certainly affords ground
for the charge that the object of Hinduism is to get
rid of conscience.

IV. HINDU ASCETICISM

The ascetic life is held in great veneration among
all Hindus, and appeals most strongly to them—a
fact which it is very important for missionaries working in India to bear in mind. Grotesque and repul-
sive as are many of the forms which it takes, no one,
we think, can fail to be impressed by the strength of
will by which a Hindu ascetic carries out his self-
inflicted torture or penance through long periods of

[1] A Hindu ascetic.

years. There have, without question, been wonderful examples of self-denial and renunciation in India,
from that of the Buddha downwards; and great
emphasis has often been laid on this aspect of
Hinduism, Western writers as well as Hindus con-
trasting it favourably with the apparent absence of
any similar effort in modern Christianity. But any
real comparison fails from the fact that Christian and
Hindu asceticism are based on totally different conceptions. To the Christian, asceticism is the training
and disciplining of the *whole* man, body, soul, and
spirit, to reach his highest development, his greatest
moral and spiritual capacity. To the Hindu, asceticism is the effort by which he endeavours to annihilate
the body, which he considers inherently evil, and by
every means in his power to sink back into that
unconscious state of absorption into the supreme
essence from which he believes that he has somehow
unfortunately emerged. The Christian ascetic, again,
aims at a life of self-discipline as a means of gaining
greater freedom for the service of mankind; the
Hindu, on the other hand, with some few exceptions,
looks on his fellow-men only as a hindrance to his
own spiritual advancement, and seeks as far as
possible to free himself from any connection with
them.

Once again, Christian asceticism has a profoundly
moral aim, the subjugation (not annihilation) of the
flesh to the obedience of the spirit—of the lower and
lawless impulses of our nature to the rule of the
divinely inspired and directed will. In other words,
it aims at enabling man to live before GOD in the

filial relation of loving and true sonship. But to the Hindu, moral conceptions are only part of that illusion from which he is ever seeking to escape; while any idea of a living relation to a personal GOD is impossible, inasmuch as the whole effort of the Hindu is to lose his consciousness by re-absorption into the supreme Being.

It is these fundamental differences in the idea of the end of the ascetic life which must always be borne in mind in instituting any comparison between the asceticism of Hinduism and that of Christianity. We would like to quote in connection with this point the following extract from the *Epiphany*, in which the subject of Hindu asceticism is treated :—

"The strong wave of pessimism which appears to be submerging German philosophic thought is, we gather, responsible for the sympathy with Oriental systems which is now so prevalent. Between the gloomy mind of Schopenhauer and the Indian philosophies of despair there is evidently much affinity. Existence, in the view of both, is an unmixed evil : it were better for man if he had not been born ; but as he has suffered that worst of misfortunes, the only thing that remains is to try to creep back somehow into the unconsciousness from which he emerged. If humanity could commit a corporate act of suicide, so much the better : any-how, the better part for each man consists in re-solutely setting to work to kill out his consciousness, as the source of all evil. The ideal sage is the self-macerating fakir, who, by a ferocious exercise of the

will, succeeds in torturing his unhappy brain out of
the so-called delusion of individuality.

"The state sought to be reached by these vision-
aries, that of trance or coma, is pretty much that
which comes naturally in a fainting-fit, or from some
undue physical depression. The late John Adding-
ton Symonds, whose biography has recently been
published, describes himself as in his youth subject
to these strange lapses into the sense of nothingness
—a kind of mental without the physical swoon. It
seems to have been connected in his case with an
exceedingly infirm and consumptive constitution.
If a physician were to diagnose the physical symp-
toms of a fakir who had brought himself to the state
of belief in his oneness with Brahma, he would no
doubt find that he had reduced his brain to a
similarly morbid condition. It is not really a high
ideal to force the body, and the mind with it, into
the abnormal state which both sometimes reach
naturally by disease: indeed, it is only a species of
prolonged suicide; and suicide, however painful, is
always an act of cowardice. The self-slayer, whether
the agony he inflicts upon himself be brief or prolonged, is equally a deserter from the ranks. The
short cut or the roundabout way are equally
illegitimate exits from life, and neither, in spite of
the fortitude exhibited, is really admirable. Which,
we would ask, exhibits the higher ideal—the life
of the *Yogi* wasted in solitary self-torture till unconsciousness is achieved, or that of JESUS of
Nazareth, Who went about doing good, and Whose
continuous sacrifice was for others, not for Himself?

"Pessimism is always paralysing, both in the East and the West. In India it has been largely responsible for the present degradation of the people by the hopeless passivity which it engenders. A world and a life which are mere *maya*[1] are obviously not worth reforming ; both may have to be endured for a time, but that is all ; and in the long run nothing, neither virtue nor vice, makes very much difference. It is by the retention of this narcotic *maya*-creed as an integral feature of its system that the Bhagavat-Gita[2] (perhaps the highest product of Hindu thought) succeeds so fatally in undermining its own ethical structure, and neutralizes its most exalted moral injunctions. Those who are seeking to regenerate India by a reversion to that which is responsible for her degeneration are only seeking to rebuild a fallen house upon the same sand. National and personal reformation must proceed from a moral impulse ; and that impulse no dreary illusion-philosophy is capable of giving.

"We should be the very last to deny the value of asceticism or of the contemplative life. Austerity, self-subjugation, an intense conviction of the deceptiveness and transitoriness of the merely material life, a piercing realization of the spiritual universe and of the divine, indwelling Presence—all these are the true marks of sanctity, qualifying men and women to be the religious benefactors of suffering

---

[1] Illusion.

[2] An eclectic system of Indian philosophy. Its author, who is unknown, is supposed to have lived in India about the second or third century A.D.

humanity, whether by fervent intercession or by
direct outward activity.   But a course of continuous
meditation on the absolute identity and nonentity of
everything and everybody, as enjoined by the teaching of Hinduism, is the very worst possible training
for such a divine work.   The more convinced a man
is of the non-existence of the world the less likely he
is to be a benefactor to it."

V.   IDOLATRY IN INDIA [1]

   " To Christian eyes the most conspicuous part of
modern Hinduism is its idolatry ; and to Christian
sentiment no other sin can be more abhorrent and
revolting.   Wherever Christianity comes into contact with idolatry, she instinctively recognizes in it
the first enemy to be overcome.   In India she finds
herself face to face with idolatry in its grossest
forms ; and amongst educated people it would seem
that she has almost overcome it.   There are very
few now of those who have come well within the
reach of Christian culture who would openly avow
themselves idolaters.   Idolatry is to all such, not
perhaps sinful always, but at all events exceedingly
irrational.

   " With such a result, so far as it goes, Christians
cannot but be well pleased.   Even granting that
those who have given up their idolatry are still
very far distant from the purity of the Christian
Faith, it is still something that GOD is not dis-
honoured before their eyes, as in former times, by

   [1] From an article published in the Oxford Mission *Quarterly
Paper* for July, 1898.

being likened to things which are the work of men's hands. But how long will this better state of things last?—that is a question which may well trouble the thoughtful. One listens to some young student's contemptuous reflections on the absurdity of idol worship, and one is inclined to think that for him at least, and for all who may have the advantage of a similar education, idolatry, even though they should consciously seek to recover the sentiment that inspired it, is an impossibility, and that as education becomes more general it must finally disappear from the country. This would be a mistake; for idolatry is not merely an error of intellect, it is a sin. It is not due, primarily, to any falseness of logic, but to a perversion of the will. It is a result primarily of a moral defect, and not an intellectual. It is, of course, an intellectual absurdity as well; but the darkened intellect which can be guilty of such an absurdity is itself the result of sin, and therefore no mere intellectual culture will ever secure men permanently against idolatry. And so the question remains, Is India being permanently rescued from idolatry or not? For our part we certainly do not believe that the mere education of the schools will ever achieve such a result. For is it not a fact of history, and a very striking fact, that amongst non-Christian nations the most philosophical have ever been the most idolatrous? The wisdom of the Egyptians in ancient times has become almost proverbial; their idolatry is no less famous nor remarkable. In spite of twenty centuries of study

the world has not yet outgrown the philosophy of
the Greeks, yet it is recorded of the most cultured
city in all Greece that when S. Paul visited it ' his
spirit was stirred in him when he saw the city wholly
given to idolatry.' And to come nearer home, was
ever people prouder of its philosophy than the
Hindus? And has any country better cause to be
ashamed of its idolatry?

" These are but instances, we believe, of an almost
universal rule. It is not in the simplicity of a
primitive age that we find religion most degraded ;
it is when nations have deteriorated morally from
the primitive standard, when the darkened intellect
has given itself up to vain speculations, that the
idea of GOD becomes gradually perverted, and superstition takes the place of the simple reverence of
earlier days.

" It is not, we repeat, the result of mere ignorance
—not, that is, of a natural, innocent, childlike
ignorance—it is the result, first of all, of a perverted
will which refuses to recognize GOD, and then of
elaborate philosophies in which the natural idea of
GOD is left out.

" How well might this be illustrated by the history
of Hinduism in the past! But our concern at
present is rather with the prospects of India in the
future ; and we ask ourselves anxiously whether
the gradual disavowal of idolatry on the part of
the educated at the present day is likely to take
effect permanently? Undoubtedly, in spite of all
the intellectual contempt which is now heaped on
idolatry, there is cause for much misgiving on this

point. For, to begin with, there are many who repudiate idolatry in word, and who yet think it no shame whatever to bow down before some monstrosity in wood or stone, and who will defend themselves by saying they do not worship the idol; only they see in it a visible manifestation of some attribute of GOD. So they bow before the four-handed *Kali*, that they may be enabled to realize the power of GOD, as they will tell you, and before *Durga*, in recognition of her kindness and benevolence. Here, then, is a large class of people who, in spite of their disavowal, are yet idolaters pure and simple. Then a large proportion, perhaps a majority of those who discard idolatry themselves, nevertheless approve of it for the common people. Such people at least have not acquired that abhorrence of idolatry as a *sin* which Christians feel. To them it is obviously nothing worse than an absurdity. But the absurdity of one age, as one knows, is only too liable to become the plausible philosophy of its successor. Idolatry was furnished with a justification in old systems of philosophy, and may be again in future schemes. The class of people we are considering afford no guarantee that their descendants, even, it may be, their logical descendants, will not be idolaters like their fathers.

"And so the question becomes important: On what grounds do the educated men of to-day (we are not now speaking of converts to Christianity) give up idolatry? The answer to that question will show whether much real progress in true religion is being made, or whether the apparent progress is delusive. Much, for instance, of this modern contempt for idolatry is no doubt due to mere scepticism, to a disbelief in the supernatural altogether. So far as this is the case, we can only look for a deeper degradation than before. For scepticism, in which the true idea of GOD is lost, is always succeeded eventually by a grosser superstition. Witness, for instance, the spiritualism of our own age. Materialistic philosophy has not succeeded in banishing the belief in the supernatural ; it has only tended to substitute in the minds of those who follow it a ridiculous spiritualism for the supernatural element in true religion. Theosophy is the true counterpart of the sceptical materialism of our century. Our age, too, has to some extent fallen into idolatry, and its idols are *Mahatmas* and the like.

"We do not believe, however, that in India mere scepticism has been the most potent influence in discrediting idolatry. Rather we believe that this result has been mainly due to a conscientious effort to recover the truth. We recognize such an effort, for instance, in Brahmoism, which, next to Christianity, represents the most considerable religious movement in India during this century. We may ask, then, Is Brahmoism, or Theism in any of its various manifestations, likely to be a permanent force working towards the final abolition of idolatry in India ? And we reply that unless Theism advances much beyond its present point there is no hope of such a result. The Theists of India have won their way back by honest effort, at the cost of considerable pain and some persecution, to the standpoint of natural religion. They have learnt once more the great truth of the Unity of GOD, and have risen to a high conception of His spirituality. But they cannot maintain themselves at this point without advancing or receding. To rest in the simplicity of a primitive piety—though until Christianity appeared this was the highest aim possible for man—is now impracticable; partly, as we may conclude, because no nation ever yet has been able to maintain itself at this point, even the Jews, whose 'genius' for religion is recognized by all, lapsing again and again into idolatry; partly because of the atmosphere of speculation in which men live; but chiefly because the higher truth of Christianity is now kept constantly before their eyes, and in the light of revelation mere natural religion cannot exist in its purity. Theism must either accept revelation or it must pay the penalty of shutting its eyes to the truth, and lapse from its own standard of truth. This is at present the position of Indian Theism. And, indeed, with all its profession of going back to the religious purity of the Vedas, Indian Theism does not really attempt the impossible work of resting on a primitive type of piety. Surrounded by rival philosophies and religions as it is, it too must have its theology. Its rejection of idolatry must be based on a principle of that theology, and that principle will work itself out, however slowly, to its logical issue.

"Let us try to see what this issue is likely to be. On what principle does Indian Theism reject idolatry? We should like to have that question

answered for us by some Theist, for we are not
ourselves quite sure of the right answer. One
answer we have heard more than once, however,
and we suppose it represents fairly accurately the
Theistic view of idolatry. It is said that GOD
being a Spirit has no form. He is infinite, and
transcends all such limits as 'form' implies. To
imagine Him under any form is to deny His infinity.
Hence, though (as we constantly hear it said)
ordinary uneducated people cannot help conceiving
of Him under some particular shape, a higher and
purer theology, which can look reality in the face,
will discard the image and worship Him simply
as He is.

"Now this, though it may be perfectly good logic,
is just one of those vain speculations which S. Paul
speaks of as the precursors of idolatry. For if the
argument be pressed, and, unless it be supplemented
by what appears to be a contradictory line of argument, it leads not to any truer conception of GOD,
but either back to Pantheism, from which the Indian
Theist is trying to escape, or else to Atheism; and
it is from Pantheism that all the polytheism and
idolatry of Hinduism start. For we must remember
that it is just as much an infringement of GOD'S
infinity (from a merely logical point of view) to
suppose that He is a Person as to conceive of Him
under any particular form; and even character, and
the attributes which are component parts of character,
all imply limitation. The logical approach of Pantheism has for its starting-point this ideal of the
infinity of GOD unchecked by any other considera-

tion. The way lies through a negation of all those
qualities which seem to be inconsistent with His
infinity, and finally of His personality, until at last a
Being is reached, impersonal, characterless, of whom
nothing whatever can be predicated, not even (Indian
philosophy, in its logical consistency, has not stopped
short of this stultifying conclusion) existence itself!
Such a being is Brahma. But being infinite, this
being is, *ex-hypothesi*, everywhere. He is everything
and at the same time nothing, and all we see in the
world is simply the manifestation of this nothingness, which is GOD. Each thing in nature is as
really GOD as the nothingness which lies behind.
Why should it not be worshipped as GOD, seeing that GOD does not exist except as manifested
in it?

"Such, we conceive, is the logical basis of Indian
idolatry. It is Theism, which has taken a Pantheistic direction, logically developed. And this is
the great danger of the Indian Theism of to-day.
It always tends to Pantheism, and thus to drift into
the old line of vain speculation which has resulted
in the vast system of idolatry which is now the
disgrace of India.

"These considerations lead us to the conclusion
that if idolatry is to be banished, the work will not
be done by the intellectual Theism of the Indian
Unitarian. Intellectual Theism must be corrected
by facts, such facts as Revelation alone can supply.
Just as science, if it trusts to *a priori* reasoning, and
does not constantly correct its conclusions by the
facts of nature, loses itself in the vain dreams of

2 E

magic, so religion, when once it begins to reason at all, unless it constantly checks its reasonings by reference to the facts of revelation, inevitably loses itself in degrading superstition. And such facts Christianity supplies. It tells us that man, being created in the image and likeness of GOD, is himself the best revelation of GOD; and that GOD was revealed in all the perfection of His nature, so far as man is able to know Him, in the Person of the one Man JESUS CHRIST. The character and Person of JESUS CHRIST is the one fact by which all our religious speculations as to the nature of GOD must be checked. By a study of His Person we shall be able to see, though not to understand, the great mystery of the Divine Personality without losing our sense of the Divine Infinity; and summed up in Him as its Divine Prototype, we shall learn to see the whole universe of things before which, in this their eternal presentment, it is no idolatry to bow down."

We have tried to give our readers some idea of "Hinduism as it is" among educated Hindus. The picture, we think, cannot be called either a bright or a hopeful one; and in spite of the present effort in Calcutta towards a revival of Hinduism, the more thoughtful men in educated Hindu society acknowledge the hopelessness of the situation. Pantheism has had a fair field in India and a long possession, and this is its result—a religion which, when it ceases to be a series of negations, becomes utterly fluid and vague; which counts the possession of any or of no creed a matter of indifference so long as there is conformity to social rules ; which shuts its eyes to the great fact of sin, and repudiates with scorn the name of "sinner"; which denies moral responsibility, in that it teaches that man does not stand in any relation to a personal and moral Being, but is controlled by fate ; which has no desire whatever for making converts, but only craves to receive the appreciation of the rest of mankind, who must of necessity (for none can be Hindus who are not born such) remain for ever outside its sacred limits.

This, and not the "ideal" which is to be found in the pages of some Western writers, is the real Hinduism of educated India ; and it does not require a very long experience of the condition of Hindu society to recognize—what the more honest and thoughtful among the educated Hindus are themselves ready to confess—the absolute inability of Hinduism to work out either the social, moral, or religious regeneration of the country.

APPENDIX

[FROM THE FIRST EDITION]

A SHORT account of the sect known as the Brahmo Somaj may be interesting to some of our readers. This sect of Indian Theists was originated by that very remarkable man the Rajah Ram Mohun Roy, a Bengali Brahman, who was born in 1774, and worked his way, partly by help of the Baptist missionaries at Serampore, out of idolatry and polytheism into an Unitarian Theistic belief. The word Brahmo is an adjective formed from Brahman, or GOD, and is equivalent to "Theistic." Somaj means "society" or "community." In order to discover the truth, he acquainted himself with the religious books of various faiths, and is said even to have acquired Greek and Hebrew. He also devoted himself to social reforms, and his denunciations of the practice of *suttee* had considerable weight with the British Government. But he never desired to dissociate himself from Hinduism; and he retained his "sacred thread"—the mark of a Brahman—to the last. In 1830 he visited England—the first to break the Hindu rule that prohibits crossing the sea—but succumbed to the climate in 1833 at Bristol, where he is buried.

The Theistic community, after his death, found a leader in Devendra Nath Tagore, a disciple of Ram Mohun Roy, who organized the society still further. This gentleman, born in 1818, is still living,[1] and is venerated as a patriarch

[1] He died in 1905.

by all sectons of the Somaj. It was he who first introduced the declaration of Theistic faith and renunciation of idolatry which is required of one joining the community.

The society continued to increase slowly, and in 1847 the important step was taken of giving up the Hindu Vedas, which hitherto had been regarded as inspired and infallible. The Somaj thus ranked itself as a rationalistic sect. The doctrine of transmigration was also abandoned.

In 1858 the Somaj took a new lease of life under the distinguished reformer, Keshub Chandra Sen. This gentleman, who had received an English education at the Presidency College, brought a new element into the society, and ardently devoted himself to the work of liberalizing and modernizing it. Much of the old Hindu atmosphere and customs were swept away. But his zeal, of course, brought him into collision with the conservative party, and in 1865 he found himself obliged to head a secession from the original society. A creed was definitely formulated, and the new community called itself the Brahmo Somaj of India, the members who were left being generally known by the title of the Adi (or ancient) Somaj. Keshub, before his conversion to Brahmoism, had belonged to the Vaishnava sect, or Vishnu worshippers, and he brought much of the emotional fervour which characterizes these devotees into the society. Great stress began now to be laid upon the emancipation and education of women, and the services of the Brahmo meeting-house were elaborated and improved.

In 1870 Keshub visited England, where he received a warm welcome from the Unitarian "churches," and some sanguine people thought from his great admiration for the character of CHRIST that he was about to become a Christian. On his return, however, he seems to have reacted in the direction of Orientalism, and to have somewhat lost his head. The claim to inspiration and autocracy was now more definitely put forward, and led to a further disruption in the society. Those who were unable to accept these new developments after a prolonged contest finally separated themselves from their leader, and formed themselves into a fresh body, upon a more democratic basis, distinguishing themselves by the name of the Sadharan or General Somaj. One very unfortunate cause of Keshub's loss of popularity was his consenting to marry his daughter to the Maharajah of Kuch Behar at an age lower than that which he himself had settled upon for the Brahmo community—a grave inconsistency which did much to injure his influence. A very considerable following, however, remained faithful to him, and the body over which he presided designated itself by the name of the "New Dispensation," and claimed to be the medium of fresh doctrinal revelations. The type of worship prevailing in this society was distinguished by its emotional and ceremonial style, dancing, in the Hindu fashion, being introduced as a divine solemnity. The seceding party, on the other hand, modelled themselves on a more puritanical basis, and, discarding the mysticism of the others, carried on the rationalistic aspect of the movement, allying themselves more and more to European and American modes of thought. On January 8, 1884, Keshub died, and, to evidence the catholicity of the movement, was first burnt and then buried, his tombstone being decorated with a trident, crescent, and cross. A committee of twelve "apostles" was appointed to carry on his work.

There are now, therefore, three Theistic sects in Calcutta, with about two hundred "churches" scattered throughout India :

The "Adi Somaj," which consists almost exclusively of the large joint family of the patriarch Devendra Nath Tagore, and has ceased to have much interest or influence.

The "New Dispensation," which retains the "church" erected by Keshub, but whose influence largely diminished at his death, though many of his followers are men of considerable earnestness and devotion. They are still distinguished by their mystical and emotional character. They have suffered much from bitter internal dissensions, and most unseemly broils have occurred in their services. Their most prominent adherent, Babu Protab Mozoomdar, has practically servered his connection with them, and set up for himself.

The third sect, the "Sadharan Somaj," has built itself a place of worship, and is, perhaps, the most progressive of the three. It appears to be the most attractive to the Hindu students, and possesses some men of real ability. Their chief leader at present is Pundit Sivanath Shastri, who has considerable oratorical power. The services are fairly well attended, especially at the yearly festival in January. They, too, however, are suffering much from internal dissensions and jealousies, especially between the reactionary and progressive parties. Their theology also fluctuates between Pantheism and Unitarianism.

All sects, however, are now distinguished by a strong animus against Christianity. The hopes formed concerning their progress towards the Faith have not been justified, though there have been individual conversions. At present both mystics and rationalists, bitterly as they are opposed, agree in repudiation of the Christian Faith, though the former party are fond of using its terminology in a fanciful and sentimental fashion. The latter have largely moulded their beliefs on Channing, Pember, Emerson, and Martineau, and have strongly imbibed their "anti-dogmatic" sentiments. Of late, Professor Caird has had considerable influence on their mode of thought.

But it is perhaps by their influence on Hindu thought and practice that the Somaj has worked most effectually.

Hindu thought has through its influence become far more Theistic, and its practice far more liberal. There is no doubt that it has held up a high ideal, both of religion and morality, and popularized many social improvements. Whatever be their ultimate destiny, the people of India will have owed much to its regenerating influence. The conceit and self-sufficiency which tends to make the society unpopular have perhaps prevented it from receiving its due meed of honour either from Hindus or Christians. We must understand that whatever victories it has achieved are really triumphs of Christianity, from which the Brahmo community has originally derived its origin.

INDEX

Argles, Rev. M. F., joins the Mission, 4; arrives in Calcutta, 6; death of, 9; notice by Canon Gore, ibid.; memorial prize, 21; Mission House chapel, a memorial to, 60.

Argles, Miss Edith, accepts the post of General Secretary, 126.

Atlay, Archdeacon, founds High School Scholarship Fund, 21.

Baptism at Torun Sen, 119 f.; of a student, 149 f.

Barber, F. W., joins the Mission, 103.

Barisal missions, previous history, 104 f.; visit of Mr. Whitehead, 106; a tour in, 108 f.; needs of, 122; Mission House in, 157; development of work at, 156; church built at, 161.

Bell, Rev. Maurice, joins the Mission, 25; invalided home, 25.

Berryman, Edwin, 4.

Bishop's College, 39, 40 f.; separation from Mission, 155.

Bow Bazaar, 5.

Brahmo Somaj, 1; welcomes the Mission, 5; intercourse with Mission, 13; see Appendix.

Brown, Rev. E. F., joins the Mission, 4; arrives in Calcutta, 5; lectures at Patna, 100; at Dacca, 100; tour in Barisal, 108 f.

Cable, Mrs., 93.

Campion, Rev. C. T., joins the Mission, 103.

Chakravarti, Jogendra Chandra, 110, 118.

Chakravarti, Shashadar, 121.

Chowdry, Rev. B. C., 54.

Clubs, Students', 30 f.

Congreve, Rev. Father, visits the Mission, 94.

Conversions, difficulties in the way of, 143 f.; persecution, 147 f.

Conway, Rev. H., joins the Mission as a layman, 41; goes to England for ordination, 92; returns to Calcutta, 102: injured in the riots, 130 f.

Cooke, Rev. J. R., joins the Mission, 103.

Copleston, Bishop, speaks of O.M. Sisterhood, 167.

Cunliffe, Mrs., 93.

Dacca, lectures at, 100; Mission House and Hostel built at, 171.

Dar, Bishan Narayan, on education in India, 79 f.

Douglas, Bishop, Charge of, 2.

Douglass, Rev. F. W., joins the Mission, 64; starts the Hostel, 86 f.

Dutt, Mrs. Khetromoni, 164.

Earthquake in Calcutta, 127 f.

Education in India, 66 f., 75 f., 79 f., 82 f., 145.

Epiphany, 13 f., 174.

Eurasians, 41, 129.

Field, Rev. W. P. G., joins the Mission, 35.

Franklin, Rev. A. E., 41, 92, 102.

Ghose, Rev. M. L., 39, 54, 95.

Gopal, 116 f.

Gore, Bishop, tribute to Rev. M. F. Argles, 9; first visit to Calcutta, 12; testimony to the Mission, 15 f.; second visit, 36; on education in India, 66 f.; opinion of the work of the *Epiphany*, 174.

High School opened, 7; scholarship fund, ibid.; enlargement, 8; moves to Bishop's College, 18; a day's routine at, 18 f.; given to the Society for the Propagation of the Gospel, 97.

Hinduism, its vagueness, 184 f.; definition of, 185 f.; its contradictions, 188 f.; a social system, 191 f.; estimate of sin, 193 f.; asceticism, 197 f.; idolatry, 202 f.; attitude of educated Hindus towards idolatry, 204 f.

Hoare, Miss, 45.

Holmes, Rev. W. H. G., joins the Mission, 173.

Hornby, Bishop, joins the Mission, 4; arrives in Calcutta, 5; Bishop of Nyasaland and afterwards Nassau, 10 note.

Hostel started by Mr. Douglass, 86; description of, 86 f.; noticed by the Government, 89; enlarged, 89; Christian students introduced, 89; converts, 170; new Hostel built, 173.

Industrial School, 38; importance of, 95; rebuilt, 96 f.; given to Oxford Mission, 97; further accounts of the work, 178.

James, St., School, 41.

Jobarpar, 168.

Johnson, Bishop, appeals to Oxford, 2; welcomes the Mission, 5; opens the Mission House, 5; urges the care of the native Christians, 6; opens the new Mission House, 57; resignation, 133.

King, Bishop, speech in 1885, 3.
King, Mrs., 60.

Langridge, Miss Edith, 166.
Liddon Lecture Hall, 58.
Lloyd, Oswald, 35; helps during the plague at Bombay, 127.

Macaulay, Lord, minute on education, 66 f.
McLaughlin, Rev. C., 132.
Manley, Rev. E., joins the Mission, 64.
Messes, students', description of, 70 f.
Moore, Rev. Father, joins the Mission, 26; work in the Sunderbans, 44; joins the Cowley Fathers, 45.
Murray, Miss, General Secretary, 17, 38, 126.
Mylne, Bishop, 172.

Nanson, Rev. W. L., Vice-Principal of Bishop's College, 102; injured in the riots, 131.
Nurses' brave conduct during the earthquake, 129.

Oxford Mission, two main principles, 3; starts in Bow Bazaar, 5; title of Brotherhood changed, 8; moves to Muktaram Babu Street, 21; daily life of, 26 f.; new Mission House, 38; opened by the Bishop, 57; description of, 57 f.; what the Mission has done, 134 f.; secret of its influence, 137.
Oxford Mission Sisterhood of the Epiphany, 166.

Pantheism, 31, 32, 190, 210.
Patna, lectures at, 99 f.
Peach, Rev. J. L., first visit to Calcutta, 12; joins the Mission, 25; takes charge of the High School, 33; Rector of St. James' School, 41.

Ringrose, Rev. R. D., 93.
Riots in Calcutta, 129 f.

Sircar, Alok, 111, 116.
Sircar, Hira Lal, 118.
Smith, Rev. P. S., joins the Mission, 12; death, 22 f.; his influence, 23 f.
Street preaching, 29.
Strong, Rev. E. L., joins the Mission, 93; develops work at Barisal, 157.
Sunderbans missions, 42; taken charge of by Oxford Mission, 43; character of the district, 46 f.; peasant life in, 48: ignorance, 50 f.

Teignmouth Shore, Rev. T. E., 171.

Thicknesse, Mr., 160, 164.

Townsend, Rev. C. W., 16, 18, 33.

Vivekananda, the Swami, 144.

Wakeman, H. O., visits the Mission, 36; gift to O.M.C. chapel, 60; death, 37 note.

Walker, Rev. C. H., joins the Mission, 16; at Bishop's College, 33; lectures at Dacca, 100.

Whitehead, Bishop, appointed to Bishop's College, 12; elected Superior of the Mis-sion, 36; on the work of Bishop's College, 40 f.; on the progress of Christianity, 63; visits to Patna, 99; visits to Barisal missions, 106; lecture on Swami Vivekananda, 144; on religious condition of the students, 147; appointed to See of Madras, 155.

Willis, Rev. E. F., joins the Mission, 4; arrives in Calcutta, 5; installed as Superior, 5; illness, 10; power of work, 10; death in England, 10.

Wilson, Sir Arthur, on education in India, 75 f.

Woodward, Rev. H. K., 41.

PRINTED BY A. R. MOWBRAY & CO. LTD.
LONDON AND OXFORD